PSYCHOANALYTIC INQUIRY

A Topical Journal for Mental Health Professionals

Volume 26 2006 Number 1

Mothers and Daughters II

ROSEMARY H. BALSAM, M.D., RUTH S. FISCHER, M.D., *Issue Editors*
Prologue 1

NANCY KULISH, PH.D.
Frida Kahlo and Object Choice: A Daughter the Rest of Her Life. 7

CORDELIA SCHMIDT-HELLERAU, PH.D.
Fighting With Spoons: On Caretaking Rivalry Between Mothers and Daughters 32

SANDRA G. HERSHBERG, M.D.
Pathways of Growth in the Mother–Daughter Relationship 56

SARALEA E. CHAZAN, PH.D.
Searching for Togetherness: The Simultaneous Treatment of a Mother and Her Early Adolescent Daughter 70

BARBARA S. SHAPIRO, M.D.
Bound Together by Chronic Pain and Trauma: A Study of Two Mother–Daughter Relationships 92

SHARON ZALUSKY, PH.D.
The Disappearing (or Ghost) Mother Transference: In Search of the Available Mother Within 118

MALKAH T. NOTMAN, M.D.
Mothers and Daughters as Adults 137

ROSEMARY H. BALSAM, M.D., RUTH S. FISCHER, M.D., *Issue Editors*
Epilogue 154

Routledge
Taylor & Francis Group
New York London

Routledge is an imprint of the
Taylor & Francis Group, an informa business

PSYCHOANALYTIC INQUIRY

Psychoanalytic Inquiry is issued 5 times a year by The Analytic Press, 810 East 10th Street, P.O. Box 1897, Lawrence, KS 66044-8897. Annual subscription rate for individuals is $93.50; for institutions, $365. Annual rate for subscribers located outside U.S.A. and Canada for individuals is $123.50; for institutions, $395. Individual issues available for $22.50 each (plus shipping & handling). Prices subject to change without notice. To order, call 800-627-0629 between 9:00 and 5:00 C.T. or write to The Analytic Press, 810 East 10th Street, P.O. Box 1897, Lawrence, KS 66044-8897.

Psychoanalytic Inquiry is accessible to subscribers online at www.analyticpress.com/onlineaccess.html.

Postmaster: Send address changes to *Psychoanalytic Inquiry,* 810 East 10th Street, Lawrence, KS 66044-8897.

Periodicals postage paid at Lawrence, KS

ISSN 0735-1690 (print)

Prologue

THIS IS THE SECOND ISSUE OF *PSYCHOANALYTIC INQUIRY* WE HAVE devoted to mothers and daughters. We began this project as the mother–daughter bond was calling out for attention in light of the many advances in our understanding of female psychology. The goal of female development is no longer considered to be a severing of the mother–daughter bond to attain autonomy and sexual maturity. What, then, are its vicissitudes as it is revisited, reworked, and transformed as the girl and her mother grow and develop and ultimately attain a state of interdependence?

We now consider the relational context of development; gender-related differences in behavior and in parental interaction; and the girl's special relationship with her mother and her mother's body and the importance to her of her own body with its special attributes, contours, and sensations.

This issue coming only a little more than a year after our first issue represents these highly experienced contemporary psychoanalytic authors' enthusiasm for contributing fresh data to this topic. Each writer illustrates how freeing and right it has been to establish that women's real-life experience turns out not to "overthrow" or psychologically need to repudiate the relationship to the mother in the radical fashion that used to be claimed was necessary to internalize and rework her own femaleness. As we said in the December 2004 issue, "For … [the girl] it is not the enduring maternal tie per se that is problematic, but rather the hampering conflicts that surround it that can diminish its effectiveness."

When a shift of a traditional concept occurs that moves us closer to truth in the lives of women (as in the articles we presented previously), a responsive creativity is released in psychoanalysis. The current authors, by further clinical and theoretical demonstrations, integrate and consolidate the grounds for these dynamics and advance our field. Further understanding and deliberations overlap from the first issue, richen the textures, and expand into new terrains.

Several of the essays begin with the familiar oppositional poles of the mother–daughter relationship: the pull to oneness and the push for autonomy. We note that we have not abandoned Mahler's insights regarding symbiosis in separation–individuation, but we offer them in a less reified form than the original, emphasizing their fertile potential for describing defensive mental states within the fantasy life of the adult. We recognize fully that the interaction of the infant girl and her mother forms a basis rather than a fixed, repeating, identical pattern for the many transformations toward adulthood.

Continuing the vicissitudes of the girl's paths toward mature sexuality, gender identity, and object choices, we have sightings of the bisexuality and fluidity that can go side by side with intimacy. Aggression is now being fully recognized as crucial in the inner life of females and no longer so avoided. Bodily pain as well as pleasure is a topic here. In this volume, there are considerations of the mother's development as well as the daughter's. Recognition that the mother herself is just as important as a subject for study as her daughter follows from a move away from the mother as a cipher as in the past and toward a new interest in a woman's development throughout the life cycle.

Metaphors and themes that represent different developmental levels show up in the essays throughout both issues. Spoons, used for gruel in the literal mutual sustenance of life between a mother and daughter in Bodenstab's 2004 contemplation on desperation in extremis during a holocaust experience, in this issue become tools for a mother and daughter to battle over female inalienable rights to nurturance. Creativity in relation to conflicts about maternal internalization is represented by Dalsimer's psychobiographical essay on the writing of Virginia Woolf in the first issue and the painting of Frida Kahlo in the second issue. Looking at the pair through movies or books in other essays also refreshes our lenses.

Marcus's 2004 piece that emphasizes the bodies of a mother and daughter as each reflect the other's potential sexuality also appears in this issue but in a more regressive layering. The daughter's adolescent reworking of the maternal internalization and its reverberations in the mother explored by Dahl in the first issue is taken up in 2006 by Hershberg. We describe other methods of studying the bond besides specifically individual analysis, such as Hoffman's 2004 account of mother–infant groups of the first issue. In this second issue, we include innovative clinical treatments of both the mother and her teenage daughter and show some new technical perspectives that have evolved. We note that the authors in the second volume reference work from the first volume, such as Notman's appreciation of Bernstein's 2004 overview of the contemporary field. Readers may or may not agree with the thinking of all these clinicians, but we hope to stimulate discussion and, therefore, growth in the field.

Nancy Kulish's psychobiography of Frida Kahlo leads off the issue. She extends her groundbreaking theoretical contribution of the Persephone complex, the myth that acknowledges a lifelong tie to the mother. The adage, "A daughter is a daughter the rest of her life" focuses us on the normal lifelong, evolving tie between mother and daughter. Kahlo, with her passionate, all-consuming relationship with her lover Diego, retained a yearning for her distant mother and for motherhood itself. Kulish demonstrates that the girl's involvement with her father as love object is understood to be an addition, a new love relationship in the girl's life added to the maternal bond but neither an abandonment nor replacement of the relationship with her mother, as old theory would have it. This significant theoretical shift allows for the complexity of multifaceted internal objects, identifications, and gender identity and is represented vividly in Kahlo's art and writings. She is presented as a woman with multiple contradictory elements who tolerated and nurtured disparity and paradox.

Cordelia Schmidt-Hellerau's "Fighting With Spoons" continues her major theoretical insight into the self-preservative drive—an underdeveloped aspect of Freud's original instinct theory that she presents as particularly apt in the life of women. She calls for a theoretical reinstatement of this drive to care for oneself and others, suggesting that had Freud been a woman, he would have more readily appreciated the importance of these elements and not dropped them so quickly. In doing so, this author notes gender differences in preservative drive activities such as the girl's earlier and greater need for attachment and greater involvement in social bonding. There are parental differences as well. Whereas mothers respond with empathic attunement, fathers do so more with agency.

In this essay, she detects three types of mothers as they partake in rivalry with their daughters over their differing needs: (1) the good-enough mother, who takes good care of self and other and gradually hands over self-preservation to her daughter; (2) the threatened mother, who is so preoccupied with her own self-preservation that she feels the child to be a menace, and, consequently, the child prematurely overdevelops object-preservative urges; and (3) the competitive mother who defends against her own neediness. In competing with her daughter as to who is the better caregiver, the competitive mother becomes overprotective.

An extensive, clarifying clinical example illustrates the technical aid provided by this understanding of self-preservative and object-preservative strivings. Awareness allows for greater discernment in differentiating the analyst's strivings from those of the patient. As the mother learns from the child, so the analyst will learn from the analysand what is needed to build a representation of optimal preservation balance between self and object.

Sandra Hershberg writes richly of the reverberations within the mother–daughter bond, noting transformations that occur at two specific transition points in the life of mother and daughter, specifically the daughter's adolescence and the mother's aging and illness. Illustrative clinical material is presented along with two films. In the first, *Freaky Friday,* mother and daughter awaken to find themselves in one another's body. In the second, *One True Thing,* the daughter must live her mother's disparaged life, which she then comes to understand and appreciate. Ultimately this leads to a more positive sense of herself as a woman and greater differentiation and autonomy. Hershberg emphasizes two poles of the interaction—empathic attunement and mutual recognition. She also conveys the crucial importance of the body. This emphasizes the frequently neglected importance of the female body with its own contours and sensations—important to both mother and daughter.

Saralea Chazan, continuing in a similar vein, explores the reverberations within the mother–daughter relationship with a focus on discerning the impingements specific to the dyad. Chazan contemplates a new therapeutic modality: simultaneous analysis of mother and child. Although this brings with it multiple complications, it does present a new perspective opening to the possibility of new discoveries. As we have become increasingly aware of the importance and effectiveness of early intervention in problematic parent–child relationships, new treatment options are welcome. Simultaneous analysis is suggested by some to be particularly useful when maladaptive boundary issues are involved. A beautiful case presentation allows the reader to gain an understanding of the therapeutic process as well as the interlocking conflicts in mother and daughter. The mother's greater comfort with her own body parallels improvement in the daughter's relationship with her mother and her body issues.

With greater self-understanding, the mother–daughter bond improved, and the mother developed a more rewarding relationship with a new man. Questions are raised about whose dynamics affect whom, the transference implications, and the importance of the father–partner or a third, in promoting growth and change in the mother–daughter bond.

The father's importance is again noted more by its marginalization, in the intense entanglement of the mother–daughter relationship in psychosomatic illness in Barbara Shapiro's article. Here, the body is the arena of expression of conflict. Shapiro applies the theoretical innovations of female psychology to her therapeutic technique with girls and women with chronic pain. Her hypothesis is that in female development, the mother–daughter relationship is so important that the widespread symptomatology in chronic body pain most likely expresses pained entanglement between mother and daughter. Two clarifying case presentations demonstrate the validity of her hypothesis. Both the adolescent patient and the mature woman illustrate an intertwining of the relations with their mothers that in turn was entwined with their psychosomatic illnesses. Intergenerational problems further intensified the mix. Shapiro demonstrates the importance of (1) not disrupting the mind–body split until enough trust is established to allow a focus on the power of emotions and (2) maintaining an alliance with the mother for the therapy to proceed.

The adult woman with chronic pain needed to keep Shapiro at a safe distance to protect her from harm, destruction, or abandonment. Warm feelings evoked a wish for and fear of merger with resulting humiliation, rage, and terror. The pain served multiple functions in dealing with this conflict over closeness and in dealing with the rage. These cases illustrate the distortion and lack of evolution of the normal push to oneness and pull to separateness that can occur as a defense against growth in the mother–daughter relationship.

Sharon Zalusky presents a case of a woman with limited ability to relate. Although in many ways quite autonomous, she was unable to allow dependency: the flip side of evolving autonomy with connectedness. The focus here is on the therapeutic challenge and the need for technical innovation when confronted with a woman with limited ability to relate. It was the patient's way of coping with the experience of her own mother as "disappearing." Because the daughter could not expect her mother to be present, she could not be devastated by her absence. It was a watertight defense. This pattern could be passed down to the next generation. Although quite successful in her career, in many ways she could not be her own agent. She would "disappear" as a person with ideas of her own. She was unable to become pregnant. As she developed the capacity to have a meaningful intimate relationship with Zalusky, she became freer to express herself and even became pregnant. She needed to trust that her analyst could cope with her independence in taking on the maternal role. Could there be more than one mother in the room? Anxiety with her new status was apparent in her inability to share the birth news with Zalusky. She regressed to her earlier sense of "I am insignificant to you. Why would you care?" The underlying fear was that her analyst could not bear her becoming a new mother. This was the importance of "not needing" her analyst as an attempt to protect against loss, abandonment, and destruction.

We chose to end this issue with Malkah Notman's fine overview that puts many of the issues that many writers are dealing with into perspective. She concentrates her remarks mostly on mothers and daughters as adults, and she has a section on ageing (an issue that analysts tackle less than other developmental stages). The article opens with the Magic Flute, illustrative of the wishes and conflicts in this pivotal mother and daughter relationship that is a worthy focus for grand opera. Notman shows the nonregressive evolving separation that is within the matrix of connection to the mother as the daughter gradually acquires mature sexuality and agency. Clinical vignettes illustrate and clarify these themes.

Dramatic social changes of the past generation are contemplated by this author. She is curious about the role of the woman's wish to conform as well as its impact on her propensity to depression. The recent focus in the literature on the importance of the female body as well as the impact of aging on the dyad is noted. Notman provides a subtly important new twist as she stresses primarily effects on the mother herself who is filled with pride, envy, competitiveness, and loss during developmental transitions in the daughter's life.

It is exciting for us to note the multiple applications and extension of the rich ideas presented in our first volume and that continue here. Through this collection of articles, we hope that our readership will feel helped and companioned in their daily thinking about the mothers and daughters with whom they are working.

Rosemary H. Balsam, M.D.
Ruth S. Fischer, M.D.
Issue Editors

Frida Kahlo and Object Choice: A Daughter the Rest of Her Life

NANCY KULISH, PH.D.

I argue that the entry into the triangular "oedipal" situation for girls does not necessitate a change in object, as Freud proposed, but an addition of object. My argument rests on different strands in contemporary psychoanalytic thinking: an appreciation of the complexity of internal objects, a reconsideration of the concept of bisexuality, an understanding of the role of multiple identifications in gender identity and object choice, and a reexamination of the triangular situation for girls. I focus on the life of Frida Kahlo—as revealed in biographies, journals, and art—to elucidate the layering of internal object choices. I conclude that object choice—heterosexual, homosexual, or bisexual—represents a composite or compromise formation.

"WHEN A MAN MARRIES HE GETS HIM A WIFE, BUT A DAUGHTER'S A daughter the rest of her life." Although this saying refers to familial relationships and the idea that a girl remains close to her mother even after she marries, it reflects the intrapsychic world as well. It implies that a daughter remains more tied to her mother internally than does a son. Indeed, psychoanalytic formulations of female development have contained such ideas that girls have more difficulty separating from their mothers and reaching sexual maturity.

According to Freud's (1908) early formulations of female development, the path into the triangular "oedipal" phase for the girl is a tortured one, starting from an inborn masculinity to a hard-won femininity. Freud believed that to find her way into the "normal" Oedipal Complex and hetero-

Nancy Kulish, Ph.D. is Adjunct Professor of Psychology, University of Detroit/Mercy; and Adjunct Assistant Professor, Department of Psychiatry, Wayne State Medical School.

sexuality, three changes must occur for the girl: of sexual organ, aim, and object. She must abandon pleasures from the "masculine" clitoris; she must convert a phallic, masculine orientation to a more passive feminine one; and finally she must renounce her original sexual object, the mother, for the father. What drives this development is the girl's discovery of sexual difference and her envy of the penis. In his 1916 "Some Character Types Met With in Psychoanalytic Work," Freud delineated the psychological consequences of the girl's penis envy: wounded narcissism, a lasting sense of inferiority, character traits of persistent jealousy, and deep resentment against her mother. I will argue that the entry into the triangular oedipal situation for girls does not necessitate a change in object, as Freud proposed, but an addition of object. That is, girls retain their desires toward their mothers, and they add other objects—male or female. This point is often missed, because libidinal attachments that girls hold toward their mothers are very often embedded and camouflaged in their attitudes and orientation toward male objects. This idea of multiple layers of internal objects or the complexity of object choice is stressed by contemporary psychoanalytic approaches.

Review of the Literature

Over the years, many psychoanalytic writers have questioned the sequence of female psychosexual development as originally laid down by Freud. In reviewing the literature, I will briefly address only those arguments that I believe have relevance for the issue of change of object. Among the important considerations are the timing of the discovery of sexual differences, the role of penis envy, the understanding of the importance of maternal identifications, considerations of bisexuality, and the nature of the female triangular situation.

Starting from the false premise that little girls' original sexuality was masculine, Freud had to find explanations for their eventual femininity and entry into the oedipal phase. His logic, in keeping with clinical observations of female envy toward men, provided an internally logical, step-by-step sequence. The first step in this progression was the girl's discovery of her "castration," her subsequent sense of lack and penis envy, resulting in her turning away from her mother in anger and disappointment and toward the father to gain compensation for her missing penis via the promise of a baby. Thus, castration impelled her into the oedipal situation but left her there. Being already "castrated," she lacked the motivation to resolve the oedipal conflicts compared with the boy. The boy's castration anxiety was formulated as what motivated him to give up his incestuous wishes, identify with his rival, the father, and move out of the oedipal phase.

A long series of psychoanalytic works, based on clinical and observational research, has challenged this sequence as erroneous and skewed (Chehrazi, 1986). To begin with, the timing of children's discovery of sexual difference is much earlier than Freud thought—eighteen months not three or four years of age (Kleeman, 1976). Thus, the discovery of the sexual difference that was thought to trigger the chain of events leading to triangulation would occur several years before the oedipal phase was thought to commence. Secondly, the role of penis envy in girl's development has been extensively rethought and reformulated. Although subsequent analysts have observed penis envy clinically, they have, from the beginning, disagreed about its primacy and its role in change of object and initiation of the Oedipus Complex. Early on, Horney (1924) asserted that the girl's inferiority complex and penis envy were secondary and culturally based. Through the years, many others have offered rich clinical understandings of the role of penis envy, which puts it in a different perspective vis à vis the developmental sequence for the girl (Lerner, 1976). Most clinicians have linked penis envy to problems the girl might have with her mother and conceptualize it not as inevitable or a necessary cog in a stepwise schema but as a passing experience in childhood. Penis envy will become prominent or fixed if there are particular forces within the family constellation, such as the birth of a baby brother, favoritism toward males, or problems in the mother–daughter relationship that reinforce it. Chasseguet-Smirgel (1970), for instance, focused on the anal–sadistic struggles between mother and daughter that nourish the girl's fantasy of mother's castrating, controlling powers and defensive idealization and envy of the paternal phallus. Frenkel (1996), in an article expressly dealing with object choice in women, presented clinical material of women and girls that demonstrated that penis envy was pathological and did not contribute to a shift in object choice to father. It is commonly agreed now that in "normal" development, the psychological consequences of penis envy that Freud originally described would more likely impede triangular development than advance it. In an influential article, Grossman and Stewart (1976) emphasized the need to analyze the meanings and functions of penis envy, when it is observed, rather than taking it as "bedrock."

Others also have questioned the inevitability of the sequence described by Freud, and further elaborated by Nagera (1975), which pictured the girl as going through a period, the so-called "negative oedipal" phase preceding the "positive oedipal" phase; that is, of first the loving mother as a phallic boy might before she turns to her father. According to Anna Freud (1965, p. 196), the negative Oedipus Complex represents a normal "homosexual" phase in the life of both boys and girls. Edgecumbe and colleagues (1976) doubted whether a negative oedipal phase is a necessary step in normal female development. In their clinical research, they found that what is described as a negative oedipal constellation may actually be considered an arrest at, or regression to, the preoedipal phallic narcissistic level characterized by dyadic object relationships.

The Kleinians, and those closely influenced by them, have offered different theories about the impetus for the male and female child's entry into the oedipal drama (Britton, et al., 1989). For them, the oedipal situation rests on a primitive unconscious awareness of the primal scene, known to the child much earlier than posited by Freud. Thus, there was no need to put forward a complicated explanation of how the girl finds her way into the oedipal situation. According to Klein (1928), primitive oedipal fantasies colored by oral sadism make their appearance in the first two years of life as a consequence of frustration by the mother. The acuteness of the ambivalence, the predominance of oral trends, and the uncertain choice of the love object characterize the Kleinian conceptualization of the very early stage of the Oedipal Complex. Segal (1974) noted the rudimentary dawning of oedipal dynamics as the infant becomes aware of the important link that exists between the father and mother. In a Kleinian tradition, Jones (1933) described very young girls' fearful fantasies of rape by their fathers, giving evidence of their projected oedipal desires.

Conversely, many analytic traditions still cling closely to essential aspects of Freud's ideas about the course of female development. Like Freud, Lacanians give primacy to the concept of a change in object. The French Lacanian analyst, Hamon (2000), posed the question, "Why do women love men and not their mothers?" The question itself reveals a theoretical assumption: that is, that girls start out with their mothers as primary objects so that there is a need to explain how they end up desiring their fathers. Hamon traced the contributions of all the early psychoanalytic pioneers to the question of the change in object for the girl and evaluated them through the lens and language of Lacanian theory. A central, defining issue for Hamon is how each theorist deals with the girl's "castration." According to

Hamon, the necessary change of object, which she takes as a given, occurs through the girl's recognition of the mother's and her own castration, her acknowledgement of the father as the bearer of the "Phallus," and submission to his "Law." I question the necessity, in the first place, of such explanations for change of object, and, in the second place, for an insistence on the role of castration in the forward movement of female development.

Contemporary Psychoanalytic Understandings of Object Choice

I now would like to draw on several different strands in contemporary psychoanalytic thinking that add further substance to the argument that object choice in females cannot be understood as a simple matter of a change from mother to father. These trends come from many sources: first, the appreciation of the complexity and multilayering of internal objects; second, the reconsideration of the concept of bisexuality; third, the role of multiple identifications in gender identity and object choice; and fourth, a reexamination of the triangular situation for girls.

The Complexity of Internal Objects

Through the intimate study of the minds of their patients in the process of psychoanalysis, psychoanalysts have come to understand the complexity of internal object representations. Arlow (1980), with his usual clarity, reminded us of this:

> From a psychological point of view the individual's concept of a person is a conglomerate of many earlier object representations. This coherent organized concept may be dissolved regressively into its antecedent object representations [p. 118]. ... The concept of the object, as well as the concept of the self and even of the superego, may undergo regressive dissolutions into their antecedent identifications. This may be observed in dreams and in psychopathology [pp. 121–122].

Thus, the final point in any individual's choice of love object—male or female—is not the entire story. Pertinent to the subject of change of object, according to this line of thought, the girl's sexual object choice of father may be built up of many earlier object representations, including maternal ones.

Young-Bruehl (2003) illuminated this complexity with clinical examples. Like Arlow, she suggested that everyone carries over varied representations of beloved familial figures into their love objects. She described four processes of transferential object choices in everyday life that contribute to the many and varied permutations of object choice:

1. Part objects: Part objects can stand for a whole object. If the part object happens to be gendered, such as a breast, then the whole object will correspondingly be gendered.
2. Split or doubled objects: Split or doubled objects are those objects onto which an individual places and separates desires once directed toward a single object. These doubled sets of objects can be male and female.
3. Composite objects: Composite objects blend parts, traits, and characteristics from at least two sources. These original sources can be objects of both genders.
4. Layered composite objects: Composite objects that are layered, for example, manifest and latent, may be male at one level and female at the other.

As Young-Bruehl stated, these fundamental processes, which can become manifest as male versus female, show up in object choice in the most varied combinations and are socially supported in complex ways (pp. 204–205).

Many contemporary writers have struggled with the question of what determines the end choice of object. Is object choice fixed in early childhood? Is it determined by biology or shaped by the environment? For Freud, object choice in women was the final outcome of a torturous set of circumstances. Problems in development could "fix" a female in a male orientation and a homosexual object choice (1931), whereas biological influences—an inborn "masculine" disposition in a girl—also could be at play (1920, pp. 169–172).

Kirkpatrick (2003) argued that sexual orientation is a "multivariate sequential determinism" and is more flexible in women. She asserted that female homosexuality does not appear to be influenced by biological factors. She pointed out that a specific gene for male homosexuality has not been found either, but rather character traits, influenced by biology, might enhance that possibility. In other words, object choice, especially for women, does not appear to be a once-and-for-all, preordained situation.

Fischer (2002) observed that the idea that the girl retains her ties to her mother as she turns toward her father can help to explain the comfort that girls and women appear to have with their bisexual inclinations as well as the emergence of homosexuality in midlife. Making another salient point, which she put succinctly: "Ties to each parent develop in tandem, not sequentially" (p. 278).

Bisexuality

As in indicated earlier, the current controversies about the "causes" for homosexuality intersect with ideas of bisexuality that have resurfaced in psychoanalytic discourse. As Young-Bruehl (2003) pointed out in a recent review of the subject, the term "bisexual" has changed meanings over time in psychoanalytic thinking. Beginning with Freud's biological bisexuality, meanings then shifted to the idea of heterosexuals or homosexuals as types of people defined by their object choices, as in Kinsey's (1948) categorizations, and now lead to a current emphasis on object choices and behaviors, which are known to be diverse, changeable, and strongly influenced by environmental factors. Young-Bruehl reviewed the research on the biological domain and concluded that none of the research has yet yielded anything that resembles a causal explanation for homosexuality or heterosexuality but that biological factors do appear to have an influence on object choice in nonspecified, indirect ways. Most researchers would also now concur that gender identity and object choice/sexual preference are not related in a simple, linear way.

Gender Identity and Object Choice

Contemporary conceptualizations of the complexity of gender identity inspire parallel careful approaches to the understanding of object choice. Balsam (2001), for example, proposed that mature gender identity in women is made up of an integrated blend of male and female identifications and bodily representations. She decried the older polarized view of female development as repudiation and overcoming masculinity. Elise (1998) adds another important voice in this discourse. She proposed that we use the term "early sense of femaleness" rather than primary femininity to keep us from reductionistic or overly simplistic thinking about female gender identity (1997). According to Elise, an early sense of a gendered self co-exists with the unconscious fantasy of potential unlimited by gender. Thus, she, like Fast (1979), would add the concept of an initial unlimited gender matrix to the Freudian bisexual matrix. She described how the individual has the possibility to reconcile—or to deny—masculinity and femininity within the self in a variety of ways. These varied somatic and cross-sex mental representations are difficult to identify beneath the surface manifestations of object representations. Thus, both Young-Bruehl and Elise have suggested that object choices are not what they appear to be on the manifest level and are composed of many conscious and unconscious layers, including bisexual components.

The Triangular Situation and Loss of Virginity

The current reformulations about female development and psychology have neglected the female triangular situation until most recently. Among the issues now being scrutinized are the idea of change of object and the girl's transition into triadic object relationships from the earlier maternal dyad.

Penis envy as the prime motivation for the girls' entry into the triadic relationship also has been questioned. Other motivations have been postulated, as outlined earlier: innate propensity to experience the primal scene (Klein, 1928), innate biological pressures, and a bisexuality from which society and family shape and guide girls typically to their fathers and lead to a suppression/repression of homosexual impulses (Butler, 1995). Whatever the explanation, penis envy is not seen by most contemporary American psychoanalysts as a satisfactory or observable explanation for girls' transition into triadic relationships. Wilkinson (1993), for example, spoke of a dress rehearsal for the triangular situation, as little girls try out blossoming sexual fantasies via masturbation first. Wilkerson followed the work of Ogden (1987) who emphasized the need for a transitional experience for the daughter to participate in an erotic relationship with another, without giving up the mother as subjective object. The girl loves the father in the mother, which is to say, the father's representation in the mother's mind. The mother, in this way, allows herself to be loved as a transitional object or substitute for the father.

Others, such as Abelin (1971) and Brown (2002), have added an account based on separation–individuation and have posited that triangulation has an earlier sequence, with the father breaking into the original dyad for both sexes and becoming a "third" for the infant. Brown (2002) proposed that there is a separate developmental line for triadic relationships. Following the Kleinian concepts, he accepts the idea of an early stage of triangularity and conflicted relations that is characterized by an early awareness and development of inner representations of the parental couple. To interpolate from these kinds of thinking, there is not a necessity, theoretically, of a change of object for the girl at the oedipal period. Instead, even in what has been called the preoedipal period, there exist primitive internal representations of father and mother. Lax (2003) added another twist to the explanation of the girl's turn to the father. She stressed the importance of the father' active role in seducing or drawing the girl to him. This is another motivational pull into heterosexuality of the triangular period for the girl.

By the same token, if castration does not get girls into the triadic situation, it does not account for their getting out of it. As Freud (1933) saw it, girls are without the motivation to develop strong superegos, which he tied to oedipal resolution and identification with the opposite parent. Although a discussion of superego development is beyond the scope of this article, I would like to say that what the early theory did not take into account or have at its disposal were the concepts of gender identity formation and of other motivations for the development of the superego, that is, ongoing identifications, throughout childhood, based on love or fear of its loss rather than fear of castration. In a contemporary reevaluation of theories of superego development, Litchenberg (2004) presented evidence that development of morality is a gradual process that entails continual additions and revisions of values and standards throughout infancy, childhood, and adulthood.

Holtzman and Kulish (2000) have argued that the girl's entry into the triangular situation differs from that originally depicted by Freud. Holtzman and Kulish take into account the pattern of little girl's typical object relationships, in comparison to the little boy's, at that period of development. These speculations derive from the work of other psychoanalytic thinkers, such as Chodorow (1978), Person (1982), Burch (1997), and Reencola (2002). Such arguments take, as their starting point, the fact that girls separate from the same-sexed object has ramifications for their further development in the triadic situation. In contrast to little boys, girls' rivals in the positive oedipal situation are of the same sex: their mothers. In the typical family constellation, girls, like boys, are very dependent on their mothers for nurture and care. Their rivalrous feelings toward their mothers are especially dangerous to their security and present a major dilemma. Hence, girls must find a way to move toward their fathers and balance those impulses with their feelings toward their mothers. Girls add rather than replace a sexual object. The situation also means that girls are particularly sensitive to issues of intimacy and to interpersonal relationships. Such arguments provide explanations for research that finds that girls' interests and values lead them more often into interpersonal domains rather than the typical abstract or spatial–motoric preoccupations of boys.

Because my colleague and I see the triangular situation for the girl as one of balancing loyalties and relationships, we (Kulish and Holtzman, 1998; Holtzman and Kulish, 2000) have called for the use of the term "Persephone Complex" rather than the oxymoron, "Female Oedipal Complex." We have proposed that the myth of Persephone and Demeter is a better fit for naming the female triangular situation—it tells the story of a girl's separation from her mother, her introduction into the adult world of sexuality, and her eventual reunion with her mother with a compromise that allows her to keep her new-found position with a man. The gods work out a compromise so that Persephone can spend part of the time with her mother and part of the time with her new husband. This story emphasizes what we have found to be true for girls, which is that they typically do not wish to leave their mothers behind as they progress through their adult development.

Burch (1997) also argued for the applicability of Persephone myth: "... the male's entry into the story ends the exclusive nature of the mother–daughter bond; henceforth the daughter's existence moves back and forth between mother and (symbolic) father. Her dilemma is that of a divided psyche, oscillating between two worlds (p. 20). ... The Demeter–Persephone narrative invites us to question whether female development is qualitatively different from male development. ... it shifts the emphasis to the task of managing complex relationships—how to continues in relationship with more than one loved person without losing the self" (p. 22). Put a little differently, the dilemma of how to preserve a relationship with more than one loved person without losing the other person is a typical conflict in the female experience.

When women and girls first enter the world of adult heterosexuality, what is on their minds is their mothers (Holtzman and Kulish, 1997). Feelings of loss and regret for a lost childhood and separation from mother are common accompaniments of this initiation of loss of virginity. This clinical finding adds support for the idea that for the girl in her entry into adult sexuality, there is an addition of object, not a change of or a renunciation of object. She holds onto her mother as she finds a new kind of relationship with a man (or another woman).

Other current writers make salient points about how girls typically give up or suppress their erotic feelings for their mothers in the course of their development. Wyre and Wells (1989) have described maternal erotic transferences, which they contend are often incompletely explored in psychoanalytic therapies. These transferences illuminate conflicted early erotic and sensual feelings, oedipal and preoedipal, of the girl toward her mother.

Case Examples

To summarize, an individual's object choice represents a composite or compromise, whether or not it results from a heterosexual, homosexual, or bisexual orientation. The little girl, in loving her "Daddy," does not give up her "Mommy." She tries to retain both in some fashion. In the case of a woman's heterosexual object choice, she typically remains close to her mother and identifies with her. Her choice of husband may very well be a compromise—the manifest picture being father–male, but a impression of the mother lies underneath. Similarly, the man's choice of an oedipal object, mother, may contain or mask the preoedipal facets. In people who are bisexual in their object choices, switching from male to female loves, this amalgam is deconstructed. Cases of a paternal object choice that masks or contains the maternal object are very familiar and frequent to most analysts.

I will present two such examples, a woman's object choice of a partner that is clearly an amalgam and a woman who seemingly tried to balance both oedipal objects.

A Case of a Composite Object Choice—Frida Kahlo

As an example of these arguments, I will offer the life of Frida Kahlo, the extraordinary Mexican artist, who has been the subject of a recent popular film *Frida* (Taymor, 2002) and a continuing source of interest for artists and art historians, feminists, and psychoanalysts. This choice to illustrate my point may seem perplexing, because Frida Kahlo appeared tied not to her mother but to her father and to her husband, the famous muralist, Diego Rivera. Nevertheless, it is for this very reason that I think a closer examination of her relationships—as revealed in her life, writings, and art—will help to elucidate the complexity and layering of her internal object choices. Although we do not have psychoanalytic data, we are fortunate in the case of Frida Kahlo to have access to many very personal and intimate writings, notebooks, and letters and to her fanciful and self-revelatory art, from which we can draw some reasonable inferences about her fantasy life. To read her diaries from the last tragic years of her life when her physical and mental health were deteriorating is to have an opening into her mind at that time.

The recent film *Frida* (Taymor, 2002) depicts the life of this extraordinary woman—"a vital force" according to Fuentes, in a forward to her diaries (Kahlo, 1995). The narrative of the film highlights her love story. After the opening shots in Kahlo's famous blue house, the film begins with a sequence showing Frida as a young girl, part of a mischievous group of adolescents (the"Cachuchas"), spying on the famous Diego Rivera having sex with one of his beautiful models. This sequence, with its primal scene impact, lays out a characterization of Diego, the great artist and womanizer; Frida, his fearless, gutsy admirer; and the future shape of their complicated, passionate, and stormy relationship. It can be taken as a paradigm of their passionate, but often sadomasochistic, relationship, bristling with jealousies and the threat of betrayal.

Kahlo's early childhood and the last tragic years before her death help to illuminate her character. To do this, I have drawn on many sources—documentaries, biographies, artistic critiques, her diary from the last 10 years of her life, and psychoanalytic writings about her. Kahlo's father was born in Germany to Hungarian Jewish parents. A head injury at 18 years old cut short a promising scholarly career and left him with epilepsy and seizures, from which he suffered all his life. He immigrated to Mexico where he became a photographer. A somewhat melancholic, bitter man, he was described as never feeling quite at ease in his adopted land. Frida clearly adored her father and identified with him and with his artistic interests. Her 1951 *Portrait of My Father* stands as testimony to her deep love for her father. She, in turn, was his favorite. Frida's mother also was of mixed ethnic origins—Indian on the paternal side and a granddaughter of a Spanish general.

Frida gathered the diverse pieces in her background and subsumed them in a love of Mexico and the mantle of her Mexican identity. She fashioned her image literally in her colorful peasant costumes, in her carefully constructed interiors of her home, and in her political embrace of Mexican nationalism and socialism. For Kahlo, this mixed ethnicity did not, as it does so often, contribute to disquiet and disharmony psychologically but rather to unquiet and dynamism. I read in her psyche not fusion or closure to aspects of the self but a mélange of contradictory elements; her art reflects this quality. Although she herself refused to be classified as a surrealist, her art contains a surrealistic and idiosyncratic mix of fantasy and realism, autobiographical and social referents, Mexican folk art, and contemporary artistic trends (Zamora, 1990; Lindauer, 1999). Frida Kahlo could tolerate disparity and paradox; in fact, she embraced it and made the most of it. I am also thinking of Kahlo's bisexual identifications, with which she appeared comfortable. As has been well documented, she had affairs with men and women, reflective of her free spirit and the Bohemian, intellectual milieu in which she moved.

Because her mother became ill shortly after Frida's birth, the infant was suckled by an Indian wet nurse. Her mother was 31 years old when Frida was born; as she approached middle age, she also began to suffer from "seizures" so that the older sisters were largely responsible for Frida's care. Frida made much of being nourished by an indigenous woman's milk and painted the wet nurse as a mythic embodiment of her Mexican heritage, as, for example, in her 1937 painting *My Nurse and I* and the 1949 painting *The Love Embrace of the Universe, the Earth {Mexico}, Me, Diego and Mr. Xolotl.* With poetic license and typical flourish, Frida, the dedicated communist, put her birth date as corresponding with the Mexican revolution, which it did not.

Some writers and psychoanalysts have speculated that this factor of her mother's unavailability laid a psychic foundation in Frida of a yearning for love and nurture and a vulnerability to loneliness. Siltala (1998), for example, traced the ambiguous and paradoxical image of the mother, infused with contrasting shadings of softness and hardness, in Kahlo's art. She hypothesized that because of the early difficulties with her mother, Kahlo's internal representation of her was diffused with anger and disappointment. Thus, through the medium of her art, she repeatedly tried to mend an image of a damaged mother. Frida's mother died in 1932 at the same time that Frida was completing the painting *My Birth.* In this painting, the mother lies on the bed, with a sheet pulled over her head, as one covers a dead body. On the wall above the bed is a painting within a painting, of the sorrowful Madonna, pierced by swords, covered with blood, a weeping Virgin of Sorrows. Kahlo often appropriated this religious imagery of the "Mater Dolorosa" tradition in Mexican art, which gives value to expression of maternal pain. Many of Kahlo's works concerned the mother–child relationship, fertility, and birth. For instance, *My Nurse and I* depicted an idealized image of a strong Mexican woman—the nurse who suckled her. In Kahlo's own words, she painted a picture "From her nipples falls milk as from the sky …" (Herrera p. 220). Yet, as Sitala points out, the nurse appears as an icon whose face is a stone mask and there is no eye contact. "The empty space—the being without—comes alongside the good experience, to be received and endured in a tension of soft and hard" (1998, p. 149).

This ambivalence toward the mother runs throughout Kahlo's life and work. It would have been difficult to please her religious, stern mother, being the girl Frida, was by nature, probably nonconforming and high spirited. It is quite plausible that Frida and her sisters would feel anxious about their mother's approval or love; she had the two older half sisters by the father's first marriage sent away to a convent when she married him, and she banished another sister from the family for several years in displeasure. The 2002 film depicts the differences between Frida and her mother in the daughter's disdain for her mother's religion and for the conventional and expected feminine role. Although Frida constantly strove to be a mother herself, she could not easily identify with or please her mother. Nevertheless, she was devastated by her mother's death. Her biographer reports that a portrait of Frida taken at this time shows "a darkness in her eyes, the unmistakable darkness of sorrow" (Herrera, 2002, p. 156).

In addition to the conflicted identifications with her mother, we can point to the abiding influence of another early trauma. At the age of six, Frida came down with polio. Sources describe her as at once being transformed from a happy, plump child to a somber thin soul. She was to spend nine months confined to her room and was left with a withered leg, which added to the continuing medical complications after her later bus accident. Because of her disfigured leg and limp from the polio, she became the object of cruel teasing by neighborhood children.

At the time of her illness, Frida developed an imaginary friend, who appears in the self-portrait *The Two Fridas*. I quote from her diary:

> On the window of my old room … I used to breathe on one of the top panes. And with my finger I would draw a door. … Through that door I would come out, in my imagination, and hurriedly, with immense happiness, I would cross all the plain I could see until I reached a

> dairy called *Pinzon*. I entered by the O of *Pinzon* and I went down into the interior of the earth, where my imaginary friend was always waiting for me. ... I do know that she was gay—she laughed a lot. She was agile and she danced as if she were weightless. I told her my secret problems [Kahlo, 1995, pp. 245–246].

Here we see the loneliness and depression of this little girl in her forced isolation, perhaps reviving the separation from her mother's breasts—she goes to a dairy that supplies milk. With this fantasy, she undoes her aloneness and her being crippled. Perhaps we can view this as a precursor of the mirrored self-images that appear and reappear in her artwork and perhaps in her choice of female sexual partners later on. What is also impressive is the child's creativity and will to master trauma by her own imagination. We see the beginnings of the efforts to invent a new, happier, and graceful persona, reinvented throughout her life. Later, when Frida put on her long Mexican costumes she repeated this story—making a statement about her Mexican identity, displaying her gaiety and her love of bright colors, and, most importantly, hiding her withered leg. She was described as laboring to make herself walk without a visible limp, gliding as it were.

Then came the horrendous life-altering accident, on top of the earlier physical trauma. A trolley plowed into the flimsy wooden bus in which Frida, then aged 17 and a student in Mexico City, and her boyfriend, Alejandro Gomez Arias, were riding. Frida was impaled by a steel rod that penetrated her pelvis and came out her vagina. Quite concretely, she was raped and left for dead by this steel rod. Her spinal column was broken in three places; her leg in eleven; her pelvis in three. Her collarbone, ribs, and foot were broken or crushed. Throughout her life, she suffered more than thirty operations, procedures, bone grafts, infections, numerous hospitalizations, plaster corsets, braces, tractions, constant back and leg pain, and finally amputation of her toes and then her bad leg, not to mention numerous miscarriages and abortions. Many of these painful medical procedures were not helpful and probably made matters worse.

A major sorrow for Frida was her inability to have a child. In spite of the physical jeopardy pregnancy and childbirth would mean for her, she repeatedly tried to become pregnant and suffered countless miscarriages and medically necessary abortions. Her preoccupation with childbirth and her sorrow over her inability to bear children runs throughout her work. For example, the famous painting *Henry Ford Hospital,* which helped to establish Kahlo as a revolutionary voice for female experience, depicted, with graphic force, the agony of her miscarriage in 1932. She wrote of her deep yearning to have Diego's baby in a letter to her doctor shortly after the miscarriage, "I had such hope to have a little Dieguito who would cry a lot" (Herrera, 2002, p. 143). She told a critic that three concerns impelled her to make art: a vivid memory of her own blood flowing during her childhood accident; her thoughts about birth, death, and the thread of life; and her desire to be a mother (Herrera, 2002, p. 319).

We might wonder why Kahlo was so intent on having a baby. Clinicians know that very often, when a girl has difficulties in identifying with her mother and the mother's role, she rejects the idea of becoming a mother herself. Certainly, this was not the case with Frida. Her strong identification with the role of mother can be discerned not only in her relentless wish for a child but also in her lifelong love of children and animals and the joy she took in teaching. Frida's intense need for having a child may also have reflected her worries about her adequacy as a female. Her early illness, her broken body, perhaps buried rivalry with a dominant mother and many sisters, a wandering husband, all called for a proof, by way of giving birth to a child, that she was a well-functioning woman.

Kahlo first began to draw from her sickbed as a child, although until the accident she had planned to go to medical school. In her art, Frida Kahlo was able to depict perhaps better than anyone the experience of her physical and emotional pain and of her female body and sexuality. Surely, as the movie and her biographies suggest, painting helped her to manage and master her pain, helplessness, and rage. As her biographer Herrera (2002) stated, "by looking at her wounded self in her paintings, Frida could sustain the illusion of being the strong, objective onlooker to her own misfortune" (p. 347). (I am not suggesting, nor do I think, that creativity can be explained as some kind of sublimation of trauma or as a mechanism of mastery over inner psychic conflicts, although any given creative individual can use her talents in these ways, as did Kahlo.)

Frida was quoted as saying that the "second great accident" in her life was Diego Rivera. When she married him, Diego Rivera was 43 years old and was Mexico's most famous artist. She was 22 years old. An infamous womanizer, Diego had had two long-term unions and countless affairs. The turbulence of their marriage is attested to by the fact that it was punctuated by a divorce and remarriage.

Frida was deeply in love with Diego, and his constant womanizing and love affairs caused her great pain. He was charismatic and was attractive to and attracted by many beautiful women. With his large ego and appetites, he could not refrain from infidelities. Frida depicted her pain about his infidelities in many of her self-portraits—a deer pierced by arrows, a self-representation with a bleeding and literally broken heart, or a self-portrait bearing a tear-stained face. After discovering Diego making love with her sister, Frida was devastated. As shown in the film *Frida* (Taymor, 2002), in her anguish and rage at his betrayal of her, she cut off her long beautiful hair that Diego loved and later painted the image of herself dressed in a man's suit—*Self Portrait with Cropped Hair* (1940). In this complex gesture, she cropped off a symbol of her vulnerable femaleness—a "castration" of her femaleness, appropriated "maleness," and took highly visible and angry vengeance on Diego. In cropping her hair, she also may have been asserting her rage at not attaining an ideal beauty or being woman enough to keep her man and bear children. The affair with her sister was especially painful, a betrayal by him and by the sister immediately younger who replaced her with her mother.

Her contemporaries, biographers, letters, diary, and her paintings all attest to her deep attachment and love for Diego. Some critics have asserted that the film *Frida* (Taymor, 2002) paid too much attention to the romance and to Diego. That may be true, but they might as well complain that Frida herself paid too much attention to Diego. I don't think Frida's love for Diego is so hard to understand, although her mother called their marriage "the mating of a dove with an elephant." Diego was the center of the universe for her and the love of her life, clearly an erotic love, as evidenced by erotic passages about Diego in her diary. In her self-portraits, such as *Diego and I* (1949), she painted Diego's face on the center of her forehead, a statement of his central importance and influence to her as an embedded introjection.

On his part, Diego found a soul mate: a woman whose art he respected. He bragged to everyone that she had a piece in the Louvre. (Diego never gained that distinction.) She shared his politics and love for Mexico. She understood him and took care of him. She loved him fiercely but could not be pushed around and from all accounts, in spite of her disabilities, or perhaps because of them, had a burning sexuality and unique attractiveness.

Kahlo herself had many affairs with powerful and famous men throughout her life—Trotsky, the sculptor Noguchi, the photographer, Nicholas Muray, and others, but none of these really captured her love. This seemingly free love was in many ways part of the scene of intelligencia in which they moved. However, her biographers and friends felt that many of the affairs were initiated in response to and as a way to cope with her feelings of rejection, jealousy, and the narcissistic wounds generated by Diego's affairs. Although the macho Diego supposedly believed in free love for himself, he could not tolerate his wife's heterosexual affairs, which she hid from him, but her relations with women apparently did not threaten him. She appeared to prefer men until late in her life, when her physical frailty made heterosexual intercourse difficult (Herrera, 2002, p. 199).[1]

We might speculate that there was another strong motive for her affairs; it appears plausible that, given her physical traumas and her triangular conflicts within her family, Frida constantly needed to strive to prove herself as an attractive woman. It is also plausible that Kahlo, in her relationships with women—and she had many close female friends—had undertones of her earlier search for mirrored self images, her unmet needs for affection from her mother, as well as her competitive and comradely relationships with her sisters. She moved easily from friendship to sexual encounter and back to friendship with men and women. Her powerful sexual appetite and sensuality permeate her art.

If we explain her turning to affairs with women in terms of "unmet maternal needs," we assume a hierarchical layering in choice of objects. That is, unsatisfied needs become a residue that does not allow for a complete "change in object" from mother to father. Preoedipal conflicts, as evidenced by bisexuality and a seemingly troubled relationship with her mother, would heighten and color her later object choice and make it difficult for her to give up her mother as primary object. Conversely, we might take another view of Kahlo's shifting love affairs from men to women to men. It can be explained more simply by the idea that, quite naturally, internal love objects are composites, mixtures, and additions, not one dimensional. If we view female development in terms of an addition of object, then Kahlo's apparent shift between male and female objects need not be seen in a negative light. Indeed, as we noted earlier, many contemporary writers have noted that women appear less constrained than do men in shifting genders of sexual object choice (Kirkpatrick, 2003) Frida Kahlo's more open psychology may allow us a view into what societal mores and

---

[1]Frida's bisexuality showed itself early. In a portrait of the family taken during her adolescence, the ever-rebellious Frida, assumes a mannish posture and wears a man's three-piece suit and tie. Her first homosexual liaison occurred during her last year at the National Preparatory School and caused a trauma. She presumably was seduced by an older woman "school teacher" (Herrera, 2002, p. 43).

individual repression have sealed over—the bisexuality in object choice and identifications that are ubiquitous.

This being said, it is important to remember that all her lovers and friends realized that they were second to Diego and could not compete with his place in her heart. One of her lovers, Nicholas Muray, wrote to Frida after she left New York for Mexico, "I knew NY only filled the bill as a temporary substitute and I hope you found your haven intact on your return. Of the three of us there was only two of you. I always felt that. Your tears told me that when you heard his voice" (Herrera, 2002, p. 269).

Diego represented for Frida many things: father and oedipal object, for he was old enough to be her father; child, for she babied him and took care of him emotionally and physically; and mother, for he fulfilled the wished-for place of the unavailable mother. The ambivalence and this yearning Frida felt toward her mother were folded into her attitudes toward Rivera. A maternal symbiotic-like meaning can be discerned in her note to Diego in her journal: "My blood is the miracle that travels in the veins of the air from my heart to yours" (Kahlo, 1995, p. 215). In another place in her journal, she wrote "Every moment, he is my child. My newborn babe, every little while, every day, of my own self" (Kahlo, 1995, p. 205). Clearly, Diego also represented a narcissistic object for her. Certainly, the two were comrades, colleagues, and friends—intellectual and artistic equals who shared the same politics and worldviews. In the film *Frida,* there is a symbolic scene in which Frida first calls Diego down from the scaffolding to her level to look at her portfolio. They had a good time with each other, that is, when they weren't making each other miserable. Diego could be a cad, narcissistic and childish, but he loved Frida above all others. He wrote, "Too late now I realized that the most wonderful part of my life had been my love for Frida" (Rivera, 1960, pp. 285–286). Observers said he became an old man all at once when she died.

In her diary, Frida movingly summed up his meanings for her: "Diego beginning, Diego, builder, Diego, my child, Diego, my boyfriend, Diego, painter, Diego, my lover, Diego, 'my husband,' Diego, my friend, Diego, my mother, Diego, my father, Diego, my son Diego = me = Universe. Diversity within unity " (Kahlo, 1995, p. 235).

Diego certainly was an oedipal object—old enough to be her father, a teacher and powerful figure, and always not quite attainable. That, I think, was part of his appeal to her. That he was an androgynous figure in other ways meant that to her he represented mother as well. Frida loved his soft, vulnerable quality and his fat man's breasts. Herrera quotes her commenting on this quality:

> Of his chest it must be said that if he had disembarked on the island governed by Sappo, he would not have been executed by the female warriors. The sensitivity of his marvelous breast would have made him admissible. Even so, his virility, specific and strange, makes him desirable also in the dominions of empresses avid for masculine love [1995, p. 370].

The aspect of Diego as mother on the one hand and child on the other is portrayed in her painting, *The Love Embrace of the Universe, the Earth Diego Me and Senior Xolotl* (1949). Frida is seated on the lap of a huge, pre-Columbian idol of a goddess. A nude baby Diego is on her lap, equal in size to her. A third eye of "supervisibility," as Kahlo wrote, is in the middle of his forehead, indicating her idealizing attitude toward him. It is striking to me that Diego's stony expression resembles that of the goddess. These three figures are set in a fantastic, organic matrix of vivid mountains and plants, desert, and jungles. Thus, Frida is caught up in an interlocking set of love embraces, one inside the other, like Russian dolls. It is as if a cosmic matrix joins and sustains her and her spouse. Years later in her diary, as she lay ill and approaching death, she scribbled to Diego:

> Only one mountain can know the core of another mountain. Your presence floats for a moment or two as if wrapping my whole being in an anxious waiting for the morning. ... For my Diego the silent life giver of worlds, what is most important is the nonillusion. Morning breaks, the friendly reds, the big blues, hands full of leaves, noisy birds, fingers in the hair, pigeons' nests—a rare understanding of human struggle simplicity of the senseless song the folly of the wind in my heart ... sweet [chocolate] of ancient Mexico [1995, pp. 216–217].

I believe that this creative, brilliant woman's freedom of expressiveness and comfort with ambiguity and paradox allowed her to communicate overtly in her words, life choices, and art what is latent in most other people. In such artistic people, who offer us their fantasies for our viewing, we can deconstruct what is carefully and tightly packed in others. What is tightly packed in others—the multilayering, or multifaceted, make-up of their internal object representations—is distinctly depicted in her art, writings, and life. To be true to Frida Kahlo, we could never speak of a "renunciation" of anything. Her psychic embrace of possibilities cannot be captured by the idea of a change from maternal love object to paternal love object, but rather an addition of object.

A Case of Mrs. L—Conflict About the Addition of an Object

Mrs. L was in her early forties and had been married for 18 years with two adolescent children. Mrs. L. came for a consultation, because she suffered from anxiety attacks and obsessive thoughts. She dated her symptoms of anxiety to right after the birth of her second child, a boy, who she felt completed their family. She could not rid herself of what appeared to be inexplicable ideas that she had made a mistake in marrying her husband and should leave him. What ran through her head were the questions that perhaps somewhere there was somebody else she should have married, although she could not imagine being married to anyone else. She could make no sense of these symptoms, because she loved her husband. She felt she and her husband were compatible, had good times together, could communicate well, and had good sex. The symptoms diminished in psychotherapy. As we discussed her marriage, it became apparent to us both that there really was not significant dissatisfaction with her husband or her marriage. Mrs. L. quickly realized that the symptoms must represent something else, something less apparent. A point to start our explorations was suggested when the anxiety symptoms flared up again after she got together for lunch with an old girlfriend who had been her best friend in high school. She recalled for me the story of her romance and marriage. She had married her husband after a quick courtship, one month after her high school sweetheart married this best friend. After she graduated and went off to college, the boyfriend began a technical school. Mrs. L would come home on some weekends to see him. Her best girlfriend went to another college in yet another town. Suddenly she discovered—she did not remember how—that on the weekends in which she didn't come home, he was going to see her girlfriend and that the two had had secret romance brewing for sometime. When the patient discovered this double betrayal, she was very upset but especially at the thought that her girlfriend would no longer be her friend. She launched an insistent campaign to keep her friendship. She drove to the other college to implore her that they remain friends. It was around the same time that she met her husband, who was several years older. At their wedding, she wanted to invite the girlfriend and ex-boyfriend, but her husband put his foot down against this. Nevertheless, she has remained friends with the girlfriend who is still married to the ex-boyfriend. Thus, it was suggestive that it was the lunch with the girlfriend stimulated the flare-up in symptoms. Mrs. L stated her belief that her husband was a much better match for her than the boyfriend would have been. In fact, her husband adored her. Perhaps this was her only complaint: his devotion made her feel guilty and unworthy, given her obsessive thoughts.

Her history was unremarkable. She felt loved by both parents and was successful in school and with her peers. She had an older brother, whom she looked up to. Her father, very good looking and a natty dresser, was very conscious of his appearance and proud of his good-looking children. During adolescence, she dressed in the baggy and campy clothes that were characteristic of the era. She recounted how her brother gave her a pair of high-heeled shoes for her sixteenth birthday. He said, "Here, you'd look really good dressing in more sexy feminine attire." From that time, as she remembers it, she wore the high heels to school with skirts and felt very good about herself. My hunch was that her older brother was a paternal figure for her, as is often the case. In this instance, his interest in her looks and sexiness was charged with oedipal significance and served as a positive stimulus in the development of a feminine identity.

The story of her boyfriend and her subsequent marriage certainly provide triangular oedipal themes ("negative" and "positive")— the proverbial love triangle and betrayal. What is striking, however, is that the primary concern was with losing her girlfriend as much as or more than her boyfriend.

This concern appears evocative of what I have argued is characteristic of the triangular situation of the little girl. As she is driven by sexual feelings toward her father and becomes jealous of her mother, she is caught in a dilemma. She is jealous of her rival, the mother. She really does not want to kill off her mother; she is afraid of losing her and needs her. She is also jealous of the father and does not want to lose her place with her mother. The Persephone myth captures this dilemma well, for it tells the tale of a girl caught in a loyalty conflict between mother and father (personified by Demeter and Hades). Thus, as the little girl, nurtured by a close, dyadic loving relationship with her mother, enters the triangular situation, she does not change sexual objects, she adds one.

At the end of adolescence Mrs. L was caught up in a Persephonal conflict. She wanted to keep her relationships with women and also have a relationship with a man for herself. It is also apparent that Mrs. L's object choice of an older man was incestuous, probably having paternal and brotherly components. Her older brother, who, with his gift of the high-heeled slippers, was a kind of fairy godmother and Prince Charming, rolled into one.

In the transference, which in this short-term treatment could not be explored in any depth, Mrs. L appeared to relate to me as a mentor or older sisterly guide. In retrospect, I suspect that she may unconsciously have put me in position of her older brother. What she came to understand was that she married her husband on the rebound, to deal with wounded pride, for "the wrong reasons," as she put it. Nevertheless, she was convinced that he was a good and appropriate choice for her. In our discussions of the events of her adolescent romance, she assumed that her behavior made sense, and it was absolutely natural to want to keep her girlfriend. She acknowledged her feelings of betrayal, but the loss of the girlfriend was more of a potential hurt. We lightly touched on the "oedipal" or "persephonal" dynamics in her choice of her husband. In fact, whenever we discussed her reasons for her choice of her husband, her thoughts would stray to her father. Thus, she gained some understanding that her obsessive thoughts about the man "she should have married" might relate to her father. Mrs. L. left treatment satisfied with her life and with her symptoms under control.

Conclusion

In their everyday clinical work, psychoanalysts know and practice this: that the internal object world is multilayered and dynamically complex. The psychoanalytic theory of female psychosexual development, in its insistence on the idea of the girl's change of object from mother to father, rather than addition of object, has stood separately from this accumulated wisdom and experience. It has also ignored the common wisdom in the saying with which I started—that "a daughter's a daughter the rest of her life."

REFERENCES

Abelin, E. (1971), The role of the father in the separation–individuation process. In: *Separation–Individuation,* ed. J. McDevitt & C. Settlage. New York: International Universities Press, pp. 229–252.

Arlow, J. (1980), Object concept and object choice, *Psychoanal. Quart.,* 49:109–133.

Balsam, R. (2001), Integrating male and female elements in a woman' gender identity, *J. Amer. Psychoanal. Assn.*, 49:1335–1361.

Britton, R., Feldman, M., & O'Shaughnessy, E. (1989), *The Oedipus Complex Today.* London: Karnak.

Brown, L. J. (2002), The early oedipal situation: Developmental, theoretical, and clinical implications, *Psychoanal. Quart.*, 71:273–300.

Burch, B. (1997), *Other Women.* New York: Columbia University Press.

Butler, J. (1995), Melancholy gender—refused identification, *Psychoanal. Dial.*, 5:165–180.

Chasseguet-Smirgel, J. (1970), Feminine guilt and the Oedipus complex. In: *Female Sexuality: New Psychoanalytic Views,* ed. J. Chassguet-Smirgel. Ann Arbor: University of Michigan Press, pp. 94–134.

Chehrazi, S. (1986), Female psychology: A review, *J. Amer. Psychoanal. Assn.*, 34:141–162.

Chodorow, N. (1978), *The Reproduction of Mothering: Psychoanalysis and the Sociology of Gender.* Berkeley: University of California Press.

Edgecumbe, R., Lunberg, S., Markowitz, R. & Salo, F. (1976), Some comments on the concept of the negative oedipal phase in girls, *The Psychoanalytic Study of the Child,* 31:35–61. New Haven, CT: Yale University Press.

Elise, D. (1997), Primary femininity, bisexuality, and the female ego ideal: A re-examination of female developmental theory, *Psychoanal. Quart.*, 66:489–517.

_____ (1998), Gender repertoire: Body, mind, and bisexuality, *Psychoanal. Dial.*, 8:353–371.

Fast, I. (1979), Developments in gender identity: gender differentiation in girls, *Internat. J. Psycho-Anal.*, 60:443–45.

Fischer, R. S. (2002), Lesbianism: Some developmental and psychodynamic considerations, *Psychoanal. Inq.*, 22:278–295.

Frenkel, R. S. (1996), A reconsideration of object choice in women: Phallus or fallacy, *J. Amer. Psychoanal. Assn.*, 44S:133–156.

Freud, A. (1965), *Normality and Pathology in Childhood: Assessments of Development.* New York: International Universities Press.

Freud, S. (1908), On the sexual theories of children. *Standard Edition,* 9:205–226, London: Hogarth Press, 1959.

_____ (1916), Some character types met with in psychoanalytic work. *Standard Edition,* 14: 309–333, London: Hogarth Press, 1957.

_____ (1920), A case of homosexuality in a woman. *Standard Edition*, 18:145–172, London: Hogarth Press, 1955.

_____ (1931), Female sexuality. *Standard Edition*, 21:221–243, London: Hogarth Press, 1961.

_____ (1933), Femininity. *Standard Editon*, 22:112–135, London: Hogarth Press, 1964.

Grossman, W. & Stewart, W. (1976), Penis envy: From childhood wish to developmental metaphor, *J. Amer. Psychoanal. Assn.,* 24 (Suppl.):193–213.

Hamon, M. (2000), *Why do Women Love Men and Not Their Mothers?* New York: Other Press.

Herrera, H. (2002), *Frida: A Biography of Frida Kahlo.* New York: HarperCollins.

Holtzman, D. & Kulish, N. (1997), *Nevermore: The Hymen and the Loss of Virginity.* Northvale, NJ: Jason Aronson, 1997.

_____ (2000), The feminization of the female oedipal complex. Part 1: A reconsideration of the significance of separation issues, *J. Amer. Psychoanal. Assn.*, 48:1413–1437.

Horney, K. (1924), On the genesis of the castration complex in women. *Internat. J. Psycho-Anal.*, 5:50–65.

Jones, E. (1933), The phallic phase. *Internat. J. Psycho-Anal.*, 14:1–13.

Kahlo, F. (1995), *The Diary of Frida Kahlo: An Intimate Self-Portrait.* New York: Abradale Press.

Kinsey, A. (1948), *Sexual Behavior in the Human Male.* Philadelphia: Saunders.

Kirkpatrick, M. (2003), The nature and nurture of gender, *Psychoanal. Inq.*, 23:558–571.

Kleeman, J. (1976), Freud's views on early female sexuality in the light of direct child observation, *J. Amer. Psychoanal. Assn.*, 24 (Suppl.):2–29.

Klein, M. (1928), Early stages of the Oedipus conflict. In: *Love, Guilt and Reparation and Other Works: The Writings of Melanie Klein, Vol. 1.* London: Hogarth Press, 1975, pp. 186–198.

Kulish, N. & Holtzman, D. (1998), Persephone, the loss of virginity and the female oedipal complex, *Internat. J. Psycho-Anal.*, 79:57–71.

Lax, R. (2003), The daughter's seduction by her father, *J. Amer. Psychoanal. Assn.*, 51:1305–1309.

Lerner, H. (1976), Parental mislabeling of female genitals as a determinant of penis envy and learning inhibitions in women, *J. Amer. Psychoanal. Assn.*, 24 (Suppl.):269–283.

Lichtenberg, J. D. (2004),Commentary on the superego—A vital or supplanted concept, *Psychoanal. Inq.*, 24:328–339.

Lindauer, M. A. (1999), *Devouring Frida: The Art History and Popular Celebrity of Frida Kahlo.* Middletown, CT: Wesleyan University Press.

Nagera, H. (1975), *Female Sexuality and the Oedipus Complex.* New York: Aronson

Ogden, T. (1987), The transitional oedipal relationship in female development, *Internat. J. Psycho-Anal.*, 68:485–498.

Person E. (1982), Women working: Fears of failure deviance and success, *J. Amer. Academy of Psychoanal.* 10:67–84.

Reencola, E. M. (2002), *The Veiled Female Core.* New York: Other Press.

Rivera, D. (1960), *My Art, My Life: An Autobiography.* New York: Citadel.

Segal, H. (1974), *Introduction to the Work of Melanie Klein.* New York: Basic Books.

Siltala, P. (1998), I made a picture of my life—As life from the picture. The life of the body in the pictures and writings of Frida Kahlo, *Internat. Forum Psychoanal.*, 7:133–155.

Taymor, J. (Director) (2002) *Frida* [Motion picture] United States: Miramax

Wilkinson, S. (1993), The female genital dress-rehearsal: A prospective process at the oedipal threshold, *Internat. J. Psycho-Anal.*, 74:313–330.

Wrye, H. & Wells, J. (1989). The maternal erotic transference, *Internat. J. Psycho-Anal.*, 70:673–684.

Young-Bruehl, E. (2003), *Where Do We Fall When We Fall In Love.* New York: Other Press

Zamora, M. (1990), *Frida Kahlo: The Brush of Anguish.* San Francisco, CA: Chronicle Books

625 Purdy
Birmingham, MI 48009
Nkulish@aol.com

Fighting With Spoons: On Caretaking Rivalry Between Mothers and Daughters

CORDELIA SCHMIDT-HELLERAU, PH.D.

I present an aspect of my version of modern drive theory with a preservative and a sexual drive as basic motivating factors in mental life. To consider self-preservation and object preservation as primal drive activities allows me to focus on the many issues of caretaking as they play a major role between mother and daughter. I discuss three different ways that mothers deal with object-preservative concerns in the interaction with the child with regard to competition and rivalry. An extended psychoanalytic example demonstrates how I use these concepts in my clinical work. The article ends with some reflections on specific countertransference difficulties in the context of self-preservative and object-preservative urges and needs.

WHAT IF FREUD HAD BEEN A WOMAN—S. FREUD: NOT SIGMUND BUT Sigrid Freud? What would psychoanalysis look like? Would we understand and conceptualize man's mind differently if it had originally been analyzed by a woman? Did Freud miss something essential from his male vantage point that needs to be added to our psychoanalytic universe? Or is it politically incorrect to ask these questions, assuming any difference in the first place?

Balsam, interested in female psychology in general (1991, 1999, 2001) and in motherhood in particular (1996, 2000, 2003), has shown how difficult it was for the first woman in the Vienna Society, Margarete Hilferding,

Cordelia Schmidt-Hellerau, Ph.D. is Training and Supervising Analyst, Swiss Psychoanalytic Society Faculty, Boston Psychoanalytic Society and Institute, The Psychoanalytic Institute of New England East, Massachusetts Institute of Psychoanalysis.

to make herself heard. The minutes of her presentation on January 11, 1911, "On the Basis of Motherlove" (Nunberg and Federn, 1974) not only tell us how disappointed Hilferding felt about the discussion of her article by her all male colleagues but also indicate that she was missing a psychoanalytic language to address certain aspects of motherhood. She struggled to think about how the body speaks in the mind of a woman. Trying to capture some of what she called "physiological motherlove," she wondered whether it was inborn or not, linked it to the issues of breast feeding and caretaking, lingered on failed motherlove, the refusal to nurse the baby, and even included cases of child abuse and murder. Freud (1905) responded with focusing on the mother's repressed infantile sexuality, very much in line with his take on the different stages of libidinal development in the *Three Essays*. However, it is striking that in one of his earliest publications, Freud (1892–1893) struggled with the same problem posed by a mother who couldn't feed her baby.

> The patient intended to feed the infant herself. ... Nevertheless, though her bodily build seemed favorable, she did not succeed. ... There was a poor flow of milk, pains were brought on when the baby was put to the breast, the mother lost appetite and showed an alarming unwillingness to take nourishment, her nights were agitated and sleepless. At last, after a fortnight, in order to avoid any further risk to the mother and infant, the attempt was abandoned as a failure and the child was transferred to a wet-nurse. Thereupon all the mother's troubles immediately cleared up [p. 117].

Freud (1892–1893), interested at that time in "antithetic ideas" and the "counterwill" treated this mother with hypnotic suggestion. At that time, even though intrigued, he was not yet capable of analyzing what was going on in his patient's mind, nor was he curious about the fact that on the occasion of this woman's second child, when the same symptoms reoccurred, his hypnosis was met with undisguised hostility. Freud noted: "Far from being welcomed as a savior in the hour of need, I was obviously being received with a bad grace and I could not count on the patient's having much confidence in me" (p. 119). Freud's hypnosis—some sort of therapeutic counterwill to the patient's anxieties—not only bypassed her defenses (which eventually led him to drop this technique in favor of psychoanalysis) but also bypassed the question that Hilferding raised nearly 20 years later and that we keep on wondering today[1]: what about motherhood is so disturbing to these women? How can we understand the specifics of neurotic derailments in motherhood and, within the particular focus of this volume, in mother–daughter relationships?

Driven to Preserve Self and Object

In my contribution to this inquiry, I want to suggest that caretaking, with all its related thoughts, fantasies, feelings, and actions, can advantageously be conceptualized as a drive activity, namely of the preservative drive (Schmidt-Hellerau, 2001, 2005). This means to reach back and to finally elaborate and explore an early conceptualization of Freud that he never made much use of. Despite the fact that he held on to the idea of self-preservation as one of the two primal drives in his theory of mental functioning,[2] it didn't appear to have ever really occurred on his male radar screen as something to think about. How could that be? It is well known that Freud thought of himself as a very masculine man, and he acknowledged difficulties with understanding female psychology. Masculinity for him appears to have been linked with the sexual—he even suggested tentatively "that libido is invariably and necessarily of a masculine nature" (1905, p. 219). Thus, Freud might have considered a preservative drive—that would, by its

[1]Of course, the history of psychoanalysis acknowledges the important contributions of women–analysts since these early days. Yet it is as if only more recently the growing number of women in our profession has led to focus anew on the specifics of female attachment, development, and separation anxieties; on women's sexuality, aggression, and superego structures; on the many shapes, functions, and languages of the female body; on maternal transferences and countertransferences; and on the bonds and conflicts between mothers and daughters (e.g., Chodorow, 1978; Silverman, 1987; Schmidt-Hellerau, 1988; Kulish 1991; Lax, 1994, 1995; Holtzman & Kulish, 1996, 1997; Kulish & Holtzman, 1998; Lax, 1999; Holtzman & Kulish, 2000; Kulish 2000, 2002; Hoffman, L., 2003; Holtzman & Kulish, 2003; Kulish & Holtzman, 2003; Balsam and Fischer, 2004; overview in Bernstein, 2004).

[2]Freud's first theory of self-preservative and sexual drives related to Darwin's theorem that self-preservation and the preservation of the species are the two success categories in the evolution of all species. Darwin's preservation of the species embraces two functions: procreation and object-preservation. Although Freud adopted the one of Darwin's categories tel quel as the "self-preservative drive," he focused for the other entirely on procreation and postulated a "sexual drive." This represented a remarkable shift for the foundations of his psychology of drives from a phenomenological–behavioral to a biological–functional perspective.

very notion, embrace all the many issues of caretaking—as necessarily of a feminine nature, a trait hardly compatible with his view of himself. At any rate, even though he did continuously quote both of his primal drives, often as hunger and love, Freud only explored the sexual drive[3] and widely ignored his self-preservative drive.

As I have elaborated in greater detail elsewhere (Schmidt-Hellerau, 2001; 2002; 2003; 2005), it is quite an amazing fact that self-preservation, man's struggle to survive, has been kept offshore in psychoanalysis for more than a hundred years.[4] In particular, because Freud changed his

---

[3]Freud focused on the "Sexuality in the Aetiology of the Neurosis" (1898); he declared the sexual infantile wish to be the main producer of our dreams (1900); he wrote the "Three Essays on Sexuality" (1905)—and never planned to write "Three Essays on Self-Preservation" (which, I think, is sorely missing today); he explored the sexual cathexis of the self in his introduction "On Narcissism" (1914); and he addressed the vicissitudes, the repression, and the unconscious of sexual wishes in his metapsychological writings of 1915.

[4]Only a few analysts have addressed this issue. Most interesting here is Ernst Simmel (1924, 1933, 1944), who elaborated on an "instinct to devour" with the goal of reassuring self-preservation and self-development; however, Simmel stayed with Freud's final decision to conceptualize the self-preservative drive together with the sexual drive as libidinal. Loewenstein (1940) focused on the self-preservative instincts, suggesting rather to call them the vital or somatic instincts. Laplanche (1997) then excludes the self-preservative drive explicitly from psychoanalytic thinking, arguing that self-preservation is a biological instinct, not a psychological drive. Khantzian and Mack (1983) elaborated extensively and most carefully on the function of self-preservation and self-care as an ego capacity. Plaut (1984) proposed to work with the concept of the "ego-instinctual drives" as a third basic drive category besides and in addition to sexuality and aggression. Modell (1985) defined narcissism as a "system for self-preservation" and proposed to view it as one causative factor of neurosis while the other remains the Oedipus complex. Silverman (1991) suggested reviving Freud's "self-preservative instincts" as an essential part of attachment behavior; she differentiated between "drives and attachment activation" (1991, p. 180), yet proposed for the latter "the same status as drives" (1991, p. 183). Quoting Freud's description of the self-preservative drives as eliciting everything that has to do "with the preservation, assertion, and magnification of the individual" (1933, p. 96) Silverman's notion of attachment as including "a need for proximity, care, and security" (1991, p. 183) emphasizes similarity. Her distinction from Freud's drives is made with regard to the object-relational aspect: attachment, as she sees it, occurs in relation to an object that "can be experienced as separate from the self," including self-objects, excluding however, "merged or nondifferentiated relationship(s)." (1991, p. 183) This latter distinction dissolves if one, as I would hold, considers the object as an integral part of Freud's drive conception. More recently, Young-Bruehl and Bethelard (1999) viewed the ego instincts as "primarily object related" (p. 838) with regard to "safety, security, caretaking, and affection" (p. 839) and suggested a "growth principle" related to the ego instincts (p. 840), analogous to the pleasure principle of the sexual instincts.

drive theory in *Beyond the Pleasure Principle* (1920), sexuality and aggression were viewed as the two basic motivating factors in mental life, whereas any notion of self-preservation was mingled with and then eclipsed by the sexual drives. However, we all are literally driven to survive. In the first months of life, we might think of the infant's self-preservative strivings as simply related to all the issues of physical well-being. Yet from the beginning, these basic needs to be taken care of (to be nursed, warm, dry and clean; to be able to breathe, digest and defecate; to feel free of pain and protected against any assault) necessarily include an object that does the caretaking. Thus the strivings of a self-preservative drive lead to building up structures in the infant's mind, representations of the caretaking dyad, within which physical and relational pleasures and meanings are combined (the pleasure of need–relief with the pleasure of the accompanying playful interactions between mother and child).

Despite his own conception that distinguished hunger from love, Freud (1905) viewed the infant's early needs and pleasures predominantly through his libidinal glasses. For instance, musing on the child's thumb sucking he writes:

> It was the child's first and most vital activity, his sucking at his mother's breast, or at substitutes for it, that must have familiarized him with this pleasure. The child's lips, in our view, behave like an erotogenic zone, and no doubt stimulation by the warm flow of milk is the cause of the pleasurable sensation. The satisfaction of the erotogenic zone is associated, in the first instance, with the satisfaction of the need for nourishment. To begin with, sexual activity attaches itself to functions serving the purpose of self-preservation and does not become independent of them until later. No one who has seen a baby sinking back satiated from the breast and falling asleep with flushed cheeks and a blissful smile can escape the reflection that this picture persists as a prototype of the expression of sexual satisfaction in later life [p. 181f].

Freud recognized that this satisfaction is about "the need for nourishment." However, the child's pleasure appears to him as sexual and is limited to the erotogenic zone of the mouth. We might not want to dismiss his idea that sexual pleasures are "attached" to the activities of the self-preservative drive. However, are there no specific pleasures of a self-preservative drive different from the sexual ones? Are the tastes of the food, the feelings of being well nourished, full and round in the stomach not pleasurable? What about the pleasures of having slept well? What about the pleasures of being well taken care of or of taking care of someone else well? What about this slight but distinctive feeling of pleasure when we finally have cleaned up our apartment, have fixed our clothes, or slip into a bed with fresh clean sheets? What about the feeling of satisfaction when we effectively warded off a serious attack?

I would state that preservative needs, and in the extreme case survival issues, are basically separate and at times even opposite to sexual strivings. As soon as we feel our life endangered—be it by an assault from the outside, by a disease, or by a deprivation of essentials to our physical health and well-being—everything else, and even the most attractive lover, is instantly pushed aside, and all we aim for is to preserve ourselves. The inheritance of Freud's focus on sexuality barred our view for a more differentiated conception, which would have enabled us to explore and conceptually grasp the many tasks, perils, confusions, and conflicts related to the strivings of a preservative drive that preoccupy us daily with making sure that we preserve ourselves and those we care about.

The fact that we are driven to care about others is an important part of the concept of a preservative drive, as I suggest it, that hasn't been recognized. Freud's rare remarks and those contributions who picked up on this concept, are all focused on and aimed at the subject, casting preservative strivings as self-centered; thus, self-preservation often appeared to be covered by the umbrella concept of narcissism. Yet as much as narcissism can (but doesn't need to) be involved in self-preservative strivings, we are not only driven to preserve ourselves (as Freud's notion self-preservative drive suggests) but also equally and powerfully driven to preserve others. Parents are driven to preserve, nurture, and protect their children[5] (not so different from any mammal's care of the brood). If

[5]A moving example for this urge to preserve the other rather than oneself can be found in Bodenstab's (2004) analysis of Rosalie's (mother) and Jolly's (daughter) interaction, when they, both near death from starvation in the concentration camp Bergen-Belsen, negotiate the sharing of a bowl of soup. Their capacity to not regress to pure self-preservation (greed) but to instead keep the object cathected—they mutually feed each other the soup—speaks of the strength of their structures (object representations) that contained and tamed their hunger and thus might have been an essential part of their psychic survival.

something or someone appears to do harm to them, they furiously interfere and fight the assault. In the same way we are all driven to help, to protect, and to take care of those who need it: our family, our friends, our colleagues, and, with varying degrees of passion, our neighbors, our citizens and our nation.

It appears to be important that we explore and reintegrate into our theory and clinical thinking this urge not only to preserve ourselves but also to preserve others. This will help us to be better aware of this important part of human strivings—and its failures—that shape our inner landscape and are an essential part of our unconscious and conscious motivations. The dual theory of preservative and sexual drives also allows us to better distinguish the libidinal strivings and cathexes of self-love and object love from the lethic strivings and cathexes of self-care and object care (I suggested the term lethe as an energy term of the preservative drive [Schmidt-Hellerau, 1997, 2001]). To put it differently: it is not the object directedness that distinguishes the drives but the specific satisfaction (their function) they are striving for that tells us what moves us in a specific fantasy, dream, anxiety, association, or action.

Gender-Specific Differences in Preservative Drive Activities

If we conceptualize self-preservation and object-preservation as primal drive activities, then we consider them to be basic for men and women alike. However, I suggest that there are important differences between the expressions of female and male preservative needs and strivings. Here our experience and intercultural observations will lead the way to what appears to be a common place: some of the basic caretaking activities—for example, nursing, cooking, feeding, cleaning, comforting, and attending to the sick, all activities inside the house—usually are performed by women, whereas building the house, hunting for food (be it in the forest or on Wall Street), and protecting the home against all kinds of dangers from the outside world are most often performed by men. This is not (or even less) specific to our modern Western culture but can be found worldwide in primitive as well as developed societies. Whether we like it or blame it on religious, social, and cultural influences, I think Freud was right when he stated that social education will not trespass beyond the lines that are laid down organically, just "impressing them somewhat more clearly and deeply" (Freud, 1905, p. 178). Compliance with gender-specific roles could not prevail in the long run if we were not—at least to a certain degree—driven to do and enjoy what we are supposed to do, if there were not these predilections that we all are so familiar with and have over the years been confirmed by scientific research.

Silverman's (1987) analysis of a great number of studies of female infants shows there is an earlier and greater need and capacity in girls for attachment to their mothers and female caregivers compared with male neonates. In addition, mothers showed a greater involvement in their interactions with infants than fathers or male caregivers even if these men were the primary caregivers. Further, female neonates show greater calm, experience earlier and longer nighttime sleep, and use feeding or diaper changing more for social bonding, whereas male infants are more cranky, easily distressed, and restless. Somewhat exaggerating we could say that the less stable and less attached state of the male infant already displays the little hunter ready to go into the world, whereas the more stable and attached female behavior indicates her predilection to develop and explore things while staying at home—and possibly clinging to mother.

From a different angle, O'Connell (2005) presents a beautiful example highlighting gender-specific differences:

> One summer my daughter, Chloe, then three years old, stepped on a bees' nest and was stung many, many times. I didn't know exactly what these stings meant to her, but she was very hurt, very frightened, and generally very stirred up. Her mother and I went about helping her in fundamentally different ways, not by design, but as you will hear, by our essential differing natures. For several nights, while the pain and distress kept her awake, my wife stayed up with Chloe, talking with her about her experience of bees, pain, surprise, fear, itching, and every other experience imaginably related to bee stings.
>
> I, on the other hand, was not content with soothing and understanding. I needed to do something. While her mother sat with her by night, I plotted with her by day. We scouted out the bees' nest and made careful, elaborate arrangements to kill the bees. Importantly, the complexity of our military operation paled in comparison to what was going on emotionally. Chloe was certainly angry at the bees, and the prospect of taking out the hive was an exciting one, but she worried about all this killing. As she once put it, "I feel angry, I feel sad, I feel

> scared, and I feel all of them A LOT!" Eventually, however, she resolved her concerns with the realization that, if we didn't get the bees, someone else was likely to get stung. Thus decided, we carried out our mission and had a great time. Many months later Chloe still talked about bees and bee stings with a bit of fear. But she also talked about killing bees with a fair bit of excitement, and a great deal of pride [p. 64f].

O'Connell characterizes the maternal response to Chloe's hurt as "nonhierarchical"; mother focused almost exclusively on the girl's needs, "instinctively matching her own agenda, rate, and rhythm to that of our child" (p. 66). By contrast, father basically set the agenda on his own and then asked his daughter to join him. Thus the maternal and paternal reactions differ in terms of their being "homeostatically attuned" or "disruptive" (Herzog, 2002).

With regard to self-preservative and object-preservative drive activities, O'Connell's example can also teach us a lot about gender-specific expressions of lethic urges. The mother, stirred up by her daughter's hurt, reacted with an increase of caretaking: her preservative actions unfolded "indoors," focused on soothing, healing, tending, and talking. While being all object preservative toward her daughter, mother was completely unaware of her own exhaustion from staying up with the little girl for three nights in a row (O'Connell, 2005, p. 66). Her object-preservative needs clearly exceeded her self-preservative concerns. Father's preservative actions instead were directed to fight back the "outdoor" enemy and thus prevent it from future assaults; by inviting Chloe to join him, his object-preservative strivings also aimed at teaching his daughter "about agency, self-protectiveness, aggression, planning, and much more." (O'Connell, 2005, p. 70) Clearly both, the female and the male way of preservative actions are indispensable for the child in the aftermath of the assault and are an important learning experience (structuring) that will help her to preserve herself and others well on her own later in life. Also very interesting is Chloe's reluctance to kill the bees; I would suggest that here she struggled with a monolithic conflict (Schmidt-Hellerau, 2005, see footnote 7) between taking revenge (self-preservation) and protecting the bees (object preservation). It was only the thought that someone else could get as badly stung by these bees as she was that helped her decide to take out the hive (any potential human victim was closer to her object-preservative needs than the insects).

All of these findings are meaningful for the issues of caretaking rivalry, because competition is always fiercest where we are driven to enjoy the same activities, as in the case of females, for example to nurture, pamper, and keep things tidy and less fierce where our urges rather complement each other, as between males and females, that is to fight and to soothe. This competition creates the specific conflicts in the area of the preservative drives between mother and daughter that is the focus of my article.

Rivalry in the Caretaker Dyad

The nursing couple is a paradigm example for a broad variety of activities that we could understand as driven by self-preservative needs (the baby) and object-preservative strivings (the mother). Although these needs and strivings are at best attuned to the baby's needs and mutually satisfying disturbances, derailments, and conflicts with self-preservation and object preservation occur in the interaction between mother and daughter on a broad spectrum between too little and too much that spans, for the infant, between deprivation and intrusion and, for the mother, between neglect and overprotection. I want to look at the interactions in the female–female caretaker dyad with a particular focus on their driven nature, and I will highlight in a very schematic way and limited to the issues at stake three different types of these interactions, which certainly does not do justice to the complexity of issues we encounter in any individual case. With a clinical example, I will then focus on rivalry between mother and daughter as it played a crucial role in my analysis with Jane.

The Good-Enough Mother A

Mother A has enough confidence in her own bodily functions. Consequently, her self-preservative strivings are healthily modulated (well structured) and feel safe. Health concerns are not a big issue on her mind. Thus, the changes of her body during pregnancy and her fantasies about giving birth are not experienced as a major threat. Also, she has already developed a mature care for the other, a sound capacity for object-preservation, is not lacking support where necessary, is not imposing help where not necessary—in short: she takes good care of herself and she cares for others. Even though mother A has the usual worries about the health of her fetus, she balances these concerns with her growing love for the fetus and delightful fantasies about a happy future of her child. When the child is born, she will enjoy taking good care of her. She doesn't do everything right and problems might occur; however, these are resolvable within her family or, if necessary, with outside help. Mother A will also gradually and appropriately hand over the tasks and challenges of self-preservation to her child, teaching her how to care for herself and eventually how to care for others. She respects and enjoys the developmental steps of her child. She is what Winnicott (1971) called the "good-enough mother."

The Threatened Mother B

Mother B feels consciously or unconsciously unsafe and threatened in her self-preservation or even her survival. (This could be a mother who was as a child overprotected or neglected and couldn't learn (structure) the tasks of self-preservation; she experiences the world as a dangerous place.) This mother might feel unconsciously threatened by all the changes in her body, with the challenges of giving birth, with pain and blood and milk. The fetus becomes a menace to her survival, the enemy within who wants to damage and kill her. (Her distress might increase when there are narcissistic issues playing into it, a resentment of becoming gross, threatening in her fantasy her capacity to attract a man, and thus ensure his support and protection and the like.) When her baby is born, she might bite her breasts, disturb her sleep, pull her nerves (see Freud's early patient). Even though she might struggle to love and nurse her baby, mother B is at least unconsciously totally preoccupied with her self-preservation in defense against her "attacker child." She tends to neglect, control (limit), or suspiciously watch and ward off the child's needs. Consequently, this child will internalize that she and her needs are a threat to her mother and that her mother is fragile and endangered. Thus her hunger will create a monolithic conflict (Schmidt-Hellerau, 2005[6]) between "I want to engulf all that I need" and "I

[6]I distinguish monolithic from binary conflicts (2005). Monolithic conflicts are usually more regressive; they involve different objects of one primal drive; for example, shall I eat all the cookies or shall I give some to my sister (preservative drive), or do I love mother or father (sexual drive)? Binary conflicts involve both primal drives and the same or different objects; for example, shall I clean my apartment or meet with my lover (different objects); shall I take care of my partner or have sex with him; shall I present myself needy or sexy (same object/self)?

need to feed everything to my mother because if she would starve I would starve as well." Sensing this dilemma, the child might prematurely develop object-preservative urges (concerns for the breast) without having established yet stable representations of a well-preserved self.

The Competitive Mother C

Consciously, mother C appears not very much concerned with her self-preservation; instead she pours all energy into object preservation. (Mother C could be a defensive version of mother B or could be the daughter of a mother B.) She is driven to care for others, anticipates all their possible needs, and finds a million ways of forestalling the efforts of others to do something on their own. Unconsciously she might be scared of wanting to be taken care of herself (self-preservative needs) and defends herself against her neediness and dependence with increased object-preservative activities that lead her to the borders of exhaustion.[7] Yet her ongoing message is this: "you don't need to do that, I can do it!" In her tireless "altruism," she competes with others in being the better caretaker. In the beginnings, her newborn is a wonderful prey to her urge to be helpful. Mother C finds total satisfaction in nursing, caring, and understanding. Her fantasy of "the perfect mother" is imperceptibly and successfully enacted as she senses with nearly uncanny empathy all her baby's needs—even before the child can feel them. She is the "overprotective mother," and soon her urge to take care of the baby will interfere and disrupt the growing infant's capacity to take over and enjoy her own self-preservative and object preservative strivings. As soon as the small child wants to do things on her own—does not want to be fed anymore but wants the spoon in her own fist to feed herself and to feed mother—this mother will say something like, "I know you want to do this now, and this is wonderful, however, you're still too little, I'll do it for you." The daughter of this mother will always be "too little," she will always be deprived of the pleasures and satisfactions of successfully performing her self-preservative and object-preservative strivings—and her relentlessly "helpful" mother will unconsciously become her greatest threat and her worst enemy.

---

[7]This is a special form of a monolithic conflict in that it is negotiated between giving (active) and receiving (passive) with the self as the central object.

There are two major outcomes: The child ends up in a state of malignant regression showing permanent helplessness, dependence, and entitlement, now demanding that mother (and all later mother substitutes) take care of her until the end of her life. Or the child doesn't give up but fights for her self-preservative and object-preservative pleasures, thus getting enmeshed in an endless circle of lethic competition. This competition goes as follows: mother C wants to feed her child with all sorts of food; however, the child pinches her lips and responds with a "vast array of no-entry defenses" (Williams, et al., 2004), or the child takes what mother gives and then throws up and spits it out. Both responses indicate mother's care is bad, doesn't nurture, but poisons the child.[8] Mother C, realizing that her food wasn't good, will increase her efforts in giving good stuff, desperately wanting to make it right, achieving the goal of being the perfect caretaker—and the daughter rejects or evacuates everything right away again and again and all over again. At the same time, the daughter too wants to care for mother, partly in an effort to repair the damage she did to her in rejecting her metaphorical milk, partly to demonstrate to mother how the good caretaking works. So the daughter too furiously tries to force something into her mother, that her mother can't take, because she wants to be the caretaker, and the child is supposed to be the one taken care of. Mother and daughter mutually want to exercise and satisfy their object-preservative drives and feel continuously interfered with and frustrated in it by the other. The situation becomes desperate when to preserve the object unconsciously means to secure ones' own self-preservation (the preservative object). From here terrible anxieties erupt and lead—often in an escalating vicious circle—to furious attacks on the one who refuses to be nurtured in order to nurture oneself.

Fighting With Spoons

Jane, a slim woman in her late thirties came to me for analysis because she continuously got into difficulties in her relationships with the women at her

[8]Williams, et al. (2004) relate a particular reason for feeding difficulties to a reversal of Bion's "container–contained" model (1962): "The infant or child is not only not contained (by the mother, addition by CSH), but is at the receiving end of parental projections. … For some, the introjection of projecting objects can become unbearable, and there is an imperative need to disgorge, emit, or block off these 'missiles'" (2004, p. xiv).

workplace and in particular with her mother. She had never married, lived on her own, and, even though doubtful, she was hoping to still find someone with whom to build a family. I remember that my first impression of Jane was mixed: on the one side, she appeared to me lively and willing to relate and change; on the other, I felt her to be highly guarded and suspicious when I said something. These first impressions would fit to what I experienced later on. Jane has a lively, colorful, creative, and funny side; she loves to surprise her friends with a nice present or to organize a birthday party with music and dance, and she is able to become excited when she does research on a complicated issue and finds a smart solution. However, Jane also has a rigid, stubborn, oppositional side to her, and at times, she was constantly preoccupied with control and power issues, which we came to struggle with a lot in the transference–countertransference occurrences.

Jane grew up in a rural area in the Midwest. She was the only child of her parents. Her mother divorced her father a few months after Jane was born, and Jane hadn't seen much of him. On the few occasions during her early childhood when her father came to visit, Jane remembered that she felt very uncomfortable. Her mother worked first as a part-time secretary and then later in a full-time position in a big company. Jane described her as often melancholic and exhausted. She worried a lot about everything, in particular about her daughter's health and whether Jane would eat enough. Jane slept with her mother in the parental bed until age 15, when she started to rebel against her mother and finally refused to sleep one more night together with her in the same room. Her adolescent years had been filled with fierce fights with her mother because Jane felt she was controlling and intruded her private space. Jane left home to go to college with some anxieties but also with much relief. After college, she had settled down on the East Coast where she found a good job and felt herself to be at a reasonable distance from her mother. However, she also loved her mother who appeared to be the only person who ever really cared for her. A year before Jane first came to see me, her aging mother had decided to move into an assisted living home only three blocks from her daughter. Jane was sympathetic with her mother's wish to be closer to her. She now wanted to show her mother more affection and provide more entertainment than she could while living far away from her. However, mother and daughter soon got into the familiar old fights that often ended in furious outbursts on Jane's side, which left both women in tears and exasperation.

During the first years of her analysis, these fights between Jane and her mother were a major issue. Jane often went over to see her mother in the evenings or on the weekends. Wanting to spoil her mother, she dragged bags of food to cook for her and spent much energy cleaning up her mother's apartment or organizing medical checkups. Yet no matter how good Jane's spirits were when doing these things, mother was always defensive, struggling with concerns that it was too much for her daughter to do all these things for her. She worried that Jane would be exhausted from the burden she put on her, and when Jane cooked for her mother, she usually ate little and urged her daughter to take the food home to use it for herself. Mother, on the other hand, also used to buy all sorts of food and wanted her daughter to drag it home. Jane felt her mother only pretended that she had meant to buy these things for herself and only later discovered that she couldn't digest them and had to give them to Jane. When Jane explicitly refused to accept, mother tried to smuggle it anyway into Jane's bags, which often led to an outburst of rage on Jane's side that made her mother cry and apologize. Also, both women competed in who would do more "good" for whom, for example, washing and creaming the other's feet, massaging the back, paying the bills in restaurants and so on, which usually ended with blaming and complaining that the other wasn't able to accept anything and wasn't appreciative of what was offered. In addition, Jane's mother would go into Jane's place and clean her kitchen or iron her blouses while Jane was working. Even though Jane had given her a key to her apartment, she hated it when her mother came in and suspected that she was going into her closets and drawers to look at what she had. All of these interactions between Jane and her mother were extremely painful—and even to listen to them was sometimes hard for me as her analyst, because all of this was presented as pure realities, and when I tried to reflect with her about what was going on, she accused me of siding with her mother—and shut down completely.

Soon our work in analysis recreated this dynamic. Our sessions revolved around the complex issues of who is giving and who is taking or who is in need of whom? Jane had different ways of talking to me: sometimes she spoke to me as if she were my boss and gave me orders in a friendly though cool manner, or she talked as if she were a mother who has everything and would gorge me with it; at other times she presented herself as dense or like a regressed child, needy and near to starving. Both sides changed rapidly. If she was in the mother position, she talked to me like to a child who doesn't know anything (e.g., describing to me in simple language and great detail certain processes at her workplace), and I would feel more stuffed than nurtured. The material itself wouldn't stimulate my analytic thinking—but, realizing this, the process did. I wondered whether Jane was feeding me with a specific (indigestible) idea of what a child needs. When I would bring this up by saying, "It is as if you need to give me so much, as if I needed a lot" Jane would agree, she did feel I wanted to hear all of this, and she did need to explain it in all detail so that I could follow her. When I would link this to her feeling of exhaustion, she would sometimes become somewhat anxious and defensive. In these moments, she was troubled by realizing that I might think differently than she did, which made her feel like a child who fears an unbearable withdrawal and separation from her mother that basically threatens her survival. Sometimes she got very anxious and agitated, as if a huge unconscious hunger had come up; then Jane would bombard me with questions and get desperate or furious if I wouldn't immediately answer to all of them.

With the following vignette I want to show how early competing self-preservative and object-preservative strivings together with changing activations of "self-as-mother" and "self-as-child" representations came up in the transference and how we tried to work on them.

Jane starts her Monday session telling me that she is very tired—first linking this to the summer's heat and then suggesting she doesn't feel like working. It's exhausting to be with people. She goes on telling me that she went to a professional meeting on Saturday, and one of her colleagues talked and talked and talked—Jane just felt like telling her to shut up. She felt insignificant in this group and didn't find much to say. Later in the evening, she had suggested to have the next meeting with a dinner at her place. One woman responded by saying, she can't eat so much in the evening. This made her mad—as if what she would serve wouldn't be good enough. She goes on telling me that she thought she'd rather make a trip to Cape Cod that day than sitting in this stupid meeting. She elaborates on that and then says, "Actually first I had thought you might have gone to the Cape, you might have a place there for the weekends—and this felt to me as if I was getting somehow into your suction—as if you were pulling me behind you."

I say: "It is my suction that pulls these thoughts out of you."

Jane says: "Well, these are my thoughts, but it is your attraction which makes these thoughts come up."

I say musing: "Suction comes from sucking."

Jane goes on: "This speaks to the vacuum that I felt on the weekend, an empty room, which I can't escape (esCape); that's why I have to follow you, but I do it reluctantly, because this suction has something devouring, it scares me. If I approached you—you would swallow me up … ”

I say: “ … because I’m so greedy.”

Jane is silent for a moment, then: “You are not greedy, but I am. Then it’s not you who wants to suck me in, it’s me. This has to do with the weekend. You didn’t see me for three days. This makes me feel that I’m not attractive enough to suck you in. I would need to have something to give that you couldn’t get elsewhere, that you would need—then you would want to see me even on the weekends.” She goes on, musing that I might have filled my weekend with paperwork, not with pleasure on the Cape. Then she says: “I wouldn’t be as patient as you are with someone like me—I’m glad you are.” Then she talks about her work and how often she feels like dumping everything. “I was exhausted on the weekend—I would have been anyway too tired to go to the Cape. I felt as if I wore lead shoes.” She sighs, pauses.

I say: “It’s tiresome to wear these lead shoes.”

Jane says: “In fact—and now I’m thinking I’m talking like my mother, she was always exhausted. I recently saw myself in a photo, and was shocked: I made the same face that my mother showed so often, tired and a little cranky. I thought I’m like my mother. There is something unresolved, something that I didn’t understand so far … ”

I say: “Maybe you are so exhausted because you feel like a little girl walking in mother’s shoes which are sooo heavy, much too heavy to go where you want to go—instead you then feel just sucked in.”

Jane says: “Hmm, an interesting thought … to be active—like yesterday when I had this exciting thought to go to the Cape—why would I be reluctant to have these thoughts. Reluctance affords a lot of energy.”

I say: “Maybe one part of you feels like little Jane who wants to go to the Cape thinking you might find me there. Yet another part feels exhausted like mother, who has to do the cooking for everybody and then is too tired to go anywhere. That puts these big lead shoes on your feet.”

Jane agrees: “That’s a good way to put it. I just thought of something else: I’m invited to a garden party in two weeks. I just wondered: how will I dress myself. There was a totally new thought: I would like to buy a hat—I have a nice dress, but no hat.” Then she goes on to tell me in a lively way about the party, how she would dance, that many of her old classmates would come—and that she even could meet an interesting man there.

Microanalysis of the Session

In this session, we had struggled with Jane's huge hunger, her need to suck me in. Her wish that I be totally attracted to her and her depressive idea that I instead didn't want to see her, appeared to reflect her feeling that she couldn't suck her mother in. It also reflects (what had been more in the center of other sessions) her narcissistic defense against acknowledging difference (the other), dependence (her need), and, at the end, the generational gap between parent and child. Thus the scary question for her always is "who sucks in whom?"

Jane had started out with a defense: she is too tired to "talk and talk and talk" (to work) with me in this session, which simultaneously states she can't give me anything and she doesn't want anything from me. On the weekend she had felt little (insignificant) at her Saturday meeting (a reversal of our no meeting) and had warded off this feeling with introducing herself as the food-providing host (mother) of the next meeting. She got mad when one colleague (child) did not appear to want to eat much. This touched on this empty room (her empty stomach, an emptiness in her mind because of my being away), which brings up her fantasy of going to the Cape—her wish to be with me. Yet this longing for me appears to stir up a dangerous devouring hunger (self-preservative); thus it is projected onto me (my suction) to better defend against: she is anyway too tired to go to the Cape (object preservative: she doesn't want to swallow and loose the nurturing mother). However, after it has become my hunger, she feels afraid: "you would swallow me up"—I suck these thoughts out of her. When I then say "because I am so greedy" I accept "the spoon" that she wants to feed me (her concern) as "my greed," I show her that this is eatable, this is digestible, and this isn't poisoned food: it is possible to acknowledge need and greed. This being said, Jane can now reject my spoon, my last "I am so greedy" interpretation (food), and interpret (feed) herself better: she can own her greed-wish to suck me in—which however, makes her feel dependent. This is worrisome, because she feels she has nothing that would guarantee that I stay with her—that she could keep me close to her. So again, she wants to be the mother rather than the baby. In this conflict between wanting to eat me up and wanting to feed me, she is stuck like in her mother's lead shoes—it is in this exhaustion that she recognizes her mother in herself. I don't interpret at that moment that she had sucked in her mother's heavy depression, thus her mother's food was in fact sickening. I stay more with her defense (wanting to be mother), her guilt (she felt her huge hunger caused this exhaustion in her mother), and her anxiety (it threatened her that her mother would withdraw/esCape). The moment when we understood in the transference that her feet express her wish to go to see me as well as her defense against it—an interpretation which appears to have been heard by Jane in a permissive sense that she could come to see me—puts a cap/hat (a limiting, containing structure) on her unlimited (greedy) self-preservative strivings, which turns the psychic movement toward libidinal fantasies: Jane gets out of her lead shoes and shifts to an enthusiastic chain of thoughts about wanting this hat for the garden party where she would dance (!) and meet a man. Even though these thoughts are clearly and affectively more libidinal—I think at this point Jane's unconscious wish to "marry" (me) is still mostly self-preservative and a wish to build with me the perfect unit of a mutually nurturing caretaking-couple.

Jane and I have mused on the question why she needs so much, why she is so deeply threatened in her survival and still has to give all the time. She tells me she was always indulged by her mother and never got the chance to learn how to do things on her own. That's why she is so afraid to lose her mother; she thinks she wouldn't be able to make it alone. She knows this isn't true, but that's how it feels. She also felt guilty for wanting so much, because her mother was tired and had to carry the burden of making a living for the two of them all by herself. Jane remembered having fantasized as a little girl that her mother would break down and she would take care of her and the little house. However, Jane also tells me how much she hated to be stuffed by her mother and how incapable her mother made her feel when Jane offered to help with cooking or cleaning, and her mother just waved her out of the room. On the one side, there is her feeling of needing to be fed; on the other side there is her wish to be the one who does the feeding without knowing how to do this. As a compromise, she has to reject what is fed, ending up with not taking in what she needs and gets (e.g., in the transference: my interpretations) and staying in this state of constantly being threatened to starve out.

Self-Preservation and Object Preservation in the Countertransference

To work with patients like Jane is a challenge to the analyst's countertransference. The patient's open or more subtle demands to be fed and provided for by her mother–analyst (more interventions, more time, and the like) create strong self-preservative and object-preservative pulls and pushes that strive to suck the analyst into an unconscious caretaking rivalry with the patient. This can become a trap or a dead end to the analysis. The difficulty is that the analyst principally wants to help. However, prolonged "feeding" help—instead of the analysis of the patient's feeling of needing to be fed—might turn into the "too-much spoon" that in the end prevents the patient from growing and even can lead to potentially malignant regressions. Further, if the analyst gives in to the demand for "feeding" help, she responds to one side of the patient's conflict, the hungry-child part (and this part—as much as the analyst might feel it—is, for a long time, unconscious), thus challenging the other side, the providing-mother part, that is an important constituent of the patient's identity ("I'm always doing everything for everybody, I'm all exhausted"). To put it differently: the patient defends herself against the child within (her frightening neediness and her overwhelming greed) with fantasizing herself in the position of a mother who controls the spoon[9]; to directly point out that she is the one who actually needs to be nurtured would bypass her defense (Busch, 1993, 2000) and most often initiate a new round of "no-entry" defenses—a patient with pinched lips.

I think to understand our wish (sometimes our impulse) to help and to provide as part of our self-preservative and object preservative strivings, as an urge that might be called up by the patient in our countertransference response, will help us to decide whether the patient needs our caretaking in a certain moment (e.g., when the patient needs to be hospitalized[10] or more metaphorically in the beginning of an analysis), or whether providing rather follows our own needs. For instance, the analyst might unconsciously be afraid of her patient's greed and then might provide to the patient (words, lowered fees, and the like) to protect herself against any possible attack (self-preservation), or the ana-

[9]I am not talking about the mother's breast and the infant's/patient's omnipotent fantasy to posses it and thus to be independed from the object. I think that these early stages that have been very well elaborated by Melanie Klein and her followers lie before, sometimes also at the bottom of what I am describing, when I'm talking about the difference between self-preservative and object-preservative strivings. This differentiation, as preliminary and incomplete as it might be, starts as it were with the baby's grabbing the spoon (see also the conflicts of seven-month-old Margaret seizing the spatula [Winnicott, 1941]).

[10]Patients who openly or in a smoldering way threaten their analysts with suicide—under this perspective—scream for a concrete object-preservative action.

lyst follows an unconscious urge to be a "good caretaker" (object preservative) instead of tolerating the transference of a bad and neglectful parent.

Most difficult, yet unavoidable, appears to me to bear and deal with the patient's "infant transference" to the analyst. I think there is a natural tendency in analysts to see themselves in mother-transference or father-transference, sometimes also in sibling-transference positions. Much more complicated are transferences that want to force the analyst into the regressive position of an infant that is to be fed and taken care of by the patient. To unconsciously defend against this demand for regression (instead of realizing and reflecting it) can limit our capacity to listen to and capture what the patient might need to tell us about how her mother–self is represented in her and what it is driven to do. For instance, the patient might act as an unempathic and at times desperate or even furious mother who wants to force into her child (the analyst) what she thinks the child needs. If the analyst clings to her own need to see herself rather in a mother-transference than in a daughter-transference, she not only misses the patient but might react with the very same "no-entry defenses" (to what she is supposed to swallow) as her patient—and both might end up in a vicious circle of caretaking rivalry (who feeds whom) that is often hard to capture right away and difficult to slowly untangle.

Whether it is about confused self-representations and object representations or about more differentiated identifications with the mother as the primary caretaker—in both cases we can ask ourselves, what is the patient driven to do and to communicate, whom is she driven to preserve in a certain moment? It is not that psychoanalysis has missed to see the neediness of the regressed or early-deprived patient. However, to capture this need as a compelling drive activity, as an urge to preserve oneself and one's objects, reveals a compelling dynamic beneath depression and aggression, an unconsciously motivated trajectory that will help us to understand the patient's ongoing open or more hidden fights with the analyst. To sort out the meaning of these urges within us, within the patient and within our interactions is a first and important step to make our interventions more acceptable and digestible for the patient. It won't always be easy to find the right words, because they all will touch on the basic threats to our survival. Yet in the end the analyst might learn from the patient like a mother learns from her child what and when and how much is needed to build up the representations of a well preserved self and object. Spoons then cease to be weapons and turn into being simply the right tools for the pleasures of a nurturing relationship.

REFERENCES

Balsam, R. H. (1991), Thinking fragments: Psychoanalysis, feminism, and postmodernism in the contemporary west, *Internat. Rev. Psycho-Anal.,* 18:128–130.

_____ (1996), The pregnant mother and the body image of the daughter, *J. Amer. Psychoanal. Assn.,* 44 (Suppl.):401–427.

_____ (1999), Becoming and being a woman, *J. Amer. Psychoanal. Assn.,* 47:266–269.

_____ (2000), The mother within the mother, *Psychoanal. Quart.,* 59:465–492.

_____ (2001), Integrating male and female elements in a woman's gender identity, *J. Amer. Psychoanal. Assn.,* 49:1335–1360.

_____ (2003), The vanished pregnant body in psychoanalytic female developmental theory, *J. Amer. Psychoanal. Assn.,* 51:1153–1179.

_____ & Fischer, R. S. (2004), Mothers and daughters, *Psychoanal. Inq.,* 24: 595–600.

Bernstein, P. (2004), Mothers and daughters from today's Psychoanalytic Perspective, *Psychoanal. Inq.,* 24:601–628.

Bodenstab, J. (2004), Under siege: A mother–daughter relationship survives the Holocaust, *Psychoanal. Inq.,* 24:731–751.

Busch, F. (1993), In the neighborhood: Aspects of a good interpretation and a developmental lag in ego-psychology, *J. Amer. Psychoanal. Assn.,* 41:151–177.

_____ (2000), What is a deep interpretation?, *J. Amer. Psychoanal. Assn.,* 48:237–254.

Bion, W. R. (1962), *Learning from Experience.* London: Heinemann.

Chodorow, N. (1978), *The Reproduction of Mothering.* Berkley: University of California Press.

Freud, S. (1892–93), A case of successful treatment by hypnotism. *Standard Edition,* 1. London: Hogarth Press, 1955.

_____ (1898), Sexuality in the aetiology of the neurosis. *Standard Edition,* 3:263–285, London: Hogarth Press, 1962.

_____ (1900), The interpretation of dreams. *Standard Edition,* 4 & 5, 1–621, London: Hogarth Press, 1953.

_____ (1905), Three essays on the theory of sexuality. *Standard Edition,* 7: 130–243, London: Hogarth Press, 1953.

_____ (1914), On narcissism: An introduction. *Standard Edition,* 14: 73–102, London: Hogarth Press, 1957.

_____ (1920), Beyond the pleasure principle. *Standard Edition,* 18: 7–64, London: Hogarth Press, 1955.

_____ (1933). New introductory lectures on psycho-analysis. *Standard Edition,* 22: 5–182, London: Hogarth Press, 1964.

Herzog, J. M. (2002), *Father Hunger.* Hillsdale, NJ: Analytic Press.

Hoffman, L. (2003), Mothers with babies and toddlers: Mastering conflicts with aggression, *J. Amer. Psychoanal. Assn.,* 51:219–1240.

Holtzman, D. & Kulish, N. (1996), The hymen and the loss of virginity, *J. Amer. Psychoanal. Assn.,* 44 (Suppl.):303–332.

_____ (1997), *The hymen and the loss of virginity.* Northvale, NJ: Aronson.

_____ (2000), The feminization of the female oedipal complex. Part I: A reconsideration of the significance of separation issues, *J. Amer. Psychoanal. Assn.,* 48:1413–1437.

_____ (2003), The feminization of the female oedipal complex. Part II: Aggression reconsidered, *J. Amer. Psychoanal. Assn.,* 51:1127–1151.

Khantzian, E. J. & Mack, J. E. (1983), Self-preservation and the care of the self—ego instincts reconsidered, *The Psychoanalytical Study of the Child,* 38:209–232. New Haven, CT: Yale University Press.

Kulish, N. (1991), The mental representation of the clitoris: The fear of female sexuality, *Psychoanal. Inq.,* 11:511–536.

_____ (2000), Primary femininity: Clinical advances and theoretical ambiguities, *J. Amer. Psychoanal. Assn.,* 48:1355–1379.

_____ (2002), Female sexuality: The pleasure of secrets and the secret of pleasure, *The Psychoanalytical Study of the Child,* 57:151–176. New Haven, CT: Yale University Press.

Kulish, N. & Holtzman, D. (1998), Persephone, the loss of virginity and the female Oedipus complex, *Internat. J. Psycho-Anal.,* 79:57–71.

_____ (2003), Countertransference and the female triangular situation, *Internat. J. Psycho-Anal.,* 84:563–577.

Laplanche, J. (1997), Le Primat de l'Autre en Psychanalyse. [The primary of the other in psychoanalysis] *Travaux* 1967–1992. Paris: Flammarion.

Lax, R. F. (1994), Aspects of primary and secondary genital feelings and anxieties in girls during the preoedipal and early oedipal phases, *Psychoanal. Quart.* 63:271–296.

_____ (1995), Freud's views and the changing perspective on femaleness and femininity, *Psychoanal. Psychol.,* 12:393–406.

_____ (1999), Nevermore: The hymen and the loss of virginity, *J. Amer. Psychoanal. Assn.,* 47:1461–1464.

Loewenstein, R. (1940), The vital or somatic instincts, *Internat. J. Psychoanal.,* 21:377–400.

Modell, A. (1985). Self preservation and the preservation of the self, *Annual of Psychoanal.,* 12/13:69–86.

Nunberg, E. & Federn, P., eds. (1974), *Minutes of the Vienna Psychoanalytic Society, Vol. 3, 1910–1911.* New York: International Universities Press.

O'Connell, M., (2005), *The Good Father. On Men, Masculinity, and Life in the Family.* New York: Scribner.

Plaut, E. A. (1984), Ego instincts: A concept whose time has come, *The Psychoanalytic Study of the Child,* 39:235–258. New Haven, CT: Yale University Press.

Schmidt-Hellerau, C. (1988), Ueber das Raetsel der Weiblichkeit. Neue Thesen zur weiblichen Entwicklung, herausgearbeitet aus dem Werk Sigmund Freuds, [The enigma of femininity. Suggestions on female development deducted from the works of Sigmund Freud.] *Psyche,* 42:289–306.

_____ (1997), Libido and lethe. Fundamentals of a formalised conception of metapsychology, *Internat. J. Psycho-Anal.,* 78:683–697.

_____ (2001), *Life Drive and Death Drive, Libido and Lethe. A Formalized Consistent Model of Psychoanalytic Drive and Structure Theory.* New York: Other Press.

_____ (2002), Why aggression? Metapsychological, clinical and technical considerations, *Internat. J. Psycho-Anal.,* 83:1269–1289.

_____ (2003). Die Erhaltung von Selbst und Objekt im Schatten der Freudschen Theorieentwicklung, [The presentation of self and object in the shadow of the development of Freud's theory] *J. Psychoanal. Theory & Practise,* 18:316–343.

_____ (2005), The other side of Oedipus. *The Psychoanalytic Quart.,* LXXIV, 187–217.

Silverman, D. K. (1987), What are little girls made of? *Psychoanal. Psychol.*, 4:315–334.

_____ (1991), Attachment patterns and Freudian theory. *Psychoanal. Psychol.*, 8:169–193.

Simmel, E. (1924), Die psycho-physische Bedeutsamkeit des Intestinalorgans fuer die Urverdraengung, [The psychophysiological meaning of the intestinal organ for primal repression] *Internat. Zschft. Psychoanalyse,* 10:218–221.

_____ (1933). Praegenitalprimat und intestinale Stufe der Libidoorganisation, [The pregenital primacy and the intestinal stage of libido organization] *Internat. Zschft. Psychoanalyse,* 19:245–246.

_____ (1944), Self-preservation and the death instinct, *Psychoanal. Quart.*, 13:160–185.

Winnicott, D. W. (1941) The observation of infants in a set situation. *Internat. J. Psycho-Anal.*, 22:229–249.

_____ (1971), *Playing and Reality*. London: Tavistock Publications Ltd.

Williams, G., Williams P., Desmarais, J. & Ravenscroft, K. (2004), Exploring Feeding Difficulties in Children. *The Generosity of Acceptance.* Vol. 1. New York: Karnac.

Young-Bruehl, E. & Bethlard, F. (1999), The Hidden History of the Ego-Instincts, *Psychoanal. Rev.*, 86(6):823–851.

246 Eliot Street
Chestnut Hill, MA 02467
drcshpd@comcast.net

Pathways of Growth in the Mother–Daughter Relationship

SANDRA G. HERSHBERG, M.D.

I focus on two central pathways of growth and change in the mother–daughter relationship—empathic attunement, which promotes a secure and cohesive sense of self, and mutual recognition of separate subjectivities, which advances differentiation of mother and daughter. A continually fluctuating balance between these two pathways of relating provides opportunities for self and mutual enhancement or possibly compromise of the relationship. Two nodal points during the life cycle, that of the daughter's adolescence and the mother's old age, are taken up through the use of film and a clinical vignette to illustrate, from a nonlinear dynamic systems theoretical perspective, movement toward maturity and transformation.

THROUGH THE DEVELOPMENTAL LENS OF NONLINEAR, DYADIC, dynamic systems theory and the use of film and a clinical vignette, I will focus on two of the paradigmatic pathways that contribute to patterns of growth and change in the mother–daughter (child) relationship, emerging and evolving throughout the life cycle. The first pathway is that of empathic attunement, postulated by Winnicott (1971), Kohut (1959, 1971, 1977, 1984), Balint (1949), and others. Emanating from a powerful desire to care for her baby (caretaking relatedness, Fosshage, 1997), the mother senses the needs of her daughter and feels both pride and preoccupation (Winnicott, 1956) in her nurturing efforts. In contrast to a traditional notion that the mother's self is subordinated to her baby, the mother's self need to

---

Sandra G. Hershberg, M.D. is a founding member and Director of Psychoanalytic Training, Institute of Contemporary Psychotherapy and Psychoanalysis, Washington, D.C. and Faculty, Washington Psychoanalytic Institute, Washington, D.C.

mother comes to the foreground in a complex interplay of shifting motivational priorities. A willingness to negotiate or subordinate other self needs is an aspect of the caregiver role, a response to her pleasure in mothering and the recognition of the attachment needs of her baby, promoting her child's developing, positive sense of self. The second pathway is that of mutual recognition between mother and child. This avenue supports the processes involved in differentiation and the appreciation of separate subjectivities (Benjamin, 1988). In my opinion, a fluctuating balance between these two modes is necessary for continued growth and change in the mother–daughter relationship.

Empathic Attunement

From the beginning, the good-enough mother "knows about the infant's needs through her identification with the infant; that is, she feels what is needed at the moment" (Winnicott, 1962, p. 70–71). In deceptively simple language, Winnicott explains the complexity of how this happens. "She (Mother) was a baby once, and she has in her memories of having been a baby; she also has memories of having been cared for, and these memories either help or hinder her in her own experience as a mother." (Davis and Walbridge, 1981, pp. 90–91) Thus, the possibility for empathic attunement of the mother depends, in part, on her positive experiences with her own good-enough mother and her ability to use these affectively and cognitively perceived symbolic and subsymbolic memories (Bucci, 2002) to provide for her baby. The mother's ability to recognize and understand disruptive patterns in the early relationship with her mother, as well as experiences with other caretakers and later relational experiences, will help her to flexibly respond to her baby's communications. Implicitly felt and not fully recognized, the mother's activated negative memories (schemas) might then be reenacted with her baby. Although the baby and child contribute their individual inputs into this mutually influenced mix, "the good-enough mother makes *active* (my emphasis) adaptation to the infant's needs" (Winnicott, 1971, p. 10). Drawing on her capacities of empathy, initiative, and imagination, the mother, as she comes to know her baby, becomes increasingly skilled in responding to her baby's needs.

In a similar fashion, Kohut speaks of the child's basic need for "an empathic environment to be in tune with her psychological need–wishes with the same unquestioning certitude as the respiratory apparatus of the newborn infant may be said to 'expect' oxygen to be contained in the surrounding atmosphere" (Kohut, 1977, p. 85) emphasizing the emotional resonance of the mother. A mother's missteps and frustrations of her baby are inevitable and, if not overly taxing to the child, also can be growth enhancing.

On a microscopic level, Lachmann (2004) and Beebe and Lachmann (2002) further refine the subprocesses, particularly in the implicit memory system, which relate to the development of the capacity for empathic attunement. Studies of mother–infant matching of temporal patterns (including vocal rhythm matching) and facial mirroring provide evidence for the way in which empathic attunement emerges as a co-constructed property of a bidirectionally interactive system. Empathic attunement, when viewed as a property of a relational field, which is highly contingent and, perhaps, paradoxically, involves a "loose coupling" between the dyad (Sander, et al., 1979) alters the field such that the infant, in a state of equilibrium, is relatively free of the pressure of internal needs and external encroachments. Thus, " … when alone—in the presence of someone—the infant can discover his own personal life" (Winnicott, 1965, p. 34).

Mutual Recognition

Benjamin's conceptualization of mutual recognition of each in the mother–baby dyad emphasizes the importance of recognition of each separate, distinct subjectivity as necessary to promote the developmental process of differentiation (and implicitly individuation). In the relational field, the growing, pleasurable, capacity of self-assertion in a milieu of recognition by the other captures, "not only the other's confirming response, but also how we find ourselves in that response," (Benjamin, 1988 p. 21) enhancing a sense of agency and efficacy. Stern's infant research (1985, 1995) indicates that the developmental achievement of sharing subjective experiences, that is, intersubjective relatedness, occurs at nine months and is highlighted by the capacity of different minds to share the same "being with" feeling, serve as underpinnings for Benjamin's ideas about intersubjectivity. Benjamin emphasizes the singular importance of subject-to-subject (compared with subject-to-object) relatedness as essential in the maturation and enhancement of separate subjectivities in ordinary development, that is, an active mutuality in which sameness and difference necessarily co-exist.

Developmental Considerations

Throughout the life cycle, situations arise that potentially can be opportunities to facilitate or to compromise the mother–daughter relationship. At various developmental junctures, the growing up daughter, identifying with and differentiating from her mother, inevitably looks toward her mother in her mind and in her life—longingly, competitively, contentiously, and compassionately (Bernstein, P., 2005). Correspondingly, "In the body of her infant daughter, a mother can see her own past self; the body is known and familiar, one with which she can have total identification" (Bernstein, D., 1983, p. 191), thus bestowing, from the mother's side, a range of implicit and explicit communications, of being female, in a full range of gendered variations.

Together mother and daughter each shape the relationship. For example, together they form patterns of interaction, patterns of being with one another, that can be self and mutually enhancing, or not. Problematic interactions may involve the daughter's sacrifice of her needs, perceptions, and experience to preserve the self-object tie, pathologically accommodating to a mother whose personal agenda has priority. In addition, the fit or mismatch of the particular pair with respect to constitutional or temperamental characteristics of each, plays a role in how smoothly interactions will proceed. From the nonlinear developmental perspective, perturbations in the continually shifting relationship occur microscopically on a moment-to-moment basis in which a change in the individual can change the relationship or vice versa, providing opportunities for self and interactional regulation (Beebe and Lachmann, 2002). On the macroscopic level, particular times of developmental transformation, such as a daughter's pregnancy, when usual patterns are shaken up, like molecules undergoing a chemical reaction and potentially forming a new equilibrium, may favor a flowering of the mother–daughter relationship, motivated by greater desire and self-examination.

I will focus on two periods in the mother–daughter relationship in greater detail, that is, the daughter's adolescence and the mother's illness or old age.

Mother–Daughter Relationship in Adolescence

In adolescence, mothers and daughters are involved in a mutually ambivalent relationship, each often struggling with her relational needs and developmental pressures. From the mother's side, she might want to enjoy the close connection with her daughter, while launching her into adulthood. From the daughter's side, she might adopt her mother as a model of womanliness, while at the same time differentiating herself from her mother to be her own person. Mother may feel threatened as she sees her daughter becoming her own person and needing less of her caretaking ministrations. Daughter may feel conflicted about her need for her mother and her mother's caretaking and her need for autonomy, her need for identification, and her need for differentiation. Feeling these conflicting pressures, in response to feeling dependent, she can become oppositional, refusing to engage in sharing of responsibility, or she can become excessively critical of the family, especially her mother, aiming not to need her mother or to disidentify with her, focusing her efforts on "how not to be like mother" (Chodorow, 1978, p. 127). At the same time, the daughter may idealize other women, teachers, friends' mothers, or very often a best friend, for example, recreating the longed for feeling of lovingness and closeness that was previously present in the mother–daughter relationship.

At a time when the daughter's body is blooming and in states of heightened sexual arousal, the mother is often on the verge of menopause, very conscious of the aging process. She may feel poignantly her body's loss of capacity to mother and question her sense of her own physical attractiveness and desirability, feeling, perhaps, a diminishment of both sexual interest and a sense of being desired, which can compromise her sense of herself. The daughter's excitement, anxiety, and confusion exists simultaneously with both her mother's pleasure in her daughter's blossoming as well as the potential for envy of her daughter's youth and beauty and critical feelings about her daughter's body. One need only remember the powerful chant of the Wicked Queen in the Snow White story, "Mirror, mirror on the wall who's the fairest of them all?" which evokes the recognition of the narcissistically injured, aging, though still beautiful, (step) mother as her daughter reaches puberty and continues to need her.

The seeming impossibility of resolution between mother and daughter at this time and the eventuality of the daughter becoming an adult woman and a mother in her own right is playfully illustrated in *Freaky Friday,* a book written by Mary Rodgers in 1972. Narrated by feisty 13-year-old Annabel Andrews, our heroine describes her plight:

> *When I woke up this morning, I found I'd turned into my mother.* There I was, in my mother's bed, with my feet reaching all the way to the bottom, and my father sleeping in the other bed. … I said to myself, "and if I have my mother's hair, I probably have her face, too." [Rodgers, 1972, p. 1, italics appear in original]

In the latest movie incarnation (Waters, 2003) a widowed therapist–mother and her 16-year-old "acting out" daughter argue about the daughter's desire to perform in her rock band on the night of her mother's engagement party. During dinner at a Chinese restaurant, the grandmotherly owner, witness to this brouhaha (impasse), casts a spell on mother and daughter, the key to the dissolution of which, is stated in a fortune cookie:

> A journey soon begins
> Its prize reflected in another's eyes
> When what you see is what you lack
> Then selfless love will bring it back [Waters, 2003]

The next scene shows "the switch" wherein each one awakens to the shock and horror of, "Eee-ew, this is not my body!" The situation of each one literally inhabiting the other's body and the terrain of the other's life creates altered, previously unexperienced, realities. This device raises the question of how to bridge (or empathize with) seemingly unbridgeable bodies and subjectivities. Can the mother move backward or can the daughter move forward to break the spell? Collaboration or "shared thirdness" (Benjamin, 2004) is necessary to break the spell.

This dyad, now bound together by the secret of "the switch," at a deeper level, harkens back to the oneness of the beginning in sharing the soft, sustaining milieu of the mother's pregnant body and forward to the daughter's transforming body and changing female representation (Balsam, 2000). The shared "secret" between mother and daughter, that of bodily transformation, emphasizes likeness in the midst of difference, the dynamic being to one which holds the possibility of greater connection and mutual need (and pleasure) in the other. In considering the adolescent girl's sexual differentiation from her mother, Bernstein (2005) moves away from the either/or of homosexual or heterosexual resolution to the more evocative notion of the adolescent's, "integrating the sensual memories of her mother's body into her own. ... Feeling in one's own body the ability to give pleasure and arouse desire evokes the dim memory of the cherished sensual softness of the mother' s body and the desires once felt toward her" (p. 620–621).

The switch concretizes a way back to the empathic position of recognizing and understanding the other. "By performing the actions of the other, we replicate their intentions within ourselves" (Benjamin, 2004, p. 19) and we are transformed. The mother's enlivened sensuality and freedom, as the daughter inhabits the mother's body, recalls the heightened sexuality of her adolescence and her current womanliness as she flirts with her daughter's boyfriend. In addition, we see the daughter's aversive, incestuous-feeling response to mother's boyfriend, who, believing she is his fiancée, attempts to kiss her. As she goes through her mother's life she, more consciously, recognizes the many demands on her mother. The mother (within her daughter's body), becomes more aware of the vulnerabilities, pressures, and conflicts her daughter faces and becomes more trusting of her daughter's version of her experiences. Further, weathering the bumps in the relationship, that is, being able to push against each other, adversarially, (Lachmann, 1986; Wolf, 1980,1988) promotes important experiences of self-assertion as attachment motivations remain in the background. Thus each feels an appreciation of their separate subjectivities and that each is doing the best she can. In this way, mother and daughter come to feel and act with the other in mind (and body), co-creating the necessary mutual recognition (Benjamin, 1988) or intersubjective relatedness (Stern, 1985), thus lifting the spell.

Clinically and personally I have been impressed that the space in which mothers and adolescent daughters have their best (perhaps only) conversations is in the car, usually when the mother is driving. In this transitional (intersubjective) space, there is a task, that is, going someplace, in the foreground. Importantly, the mother is not looking directly at her daughter, providing an arrangement of less focused attention, which alleviates the self-conscious daughter's expectancy of feeling scrutinized and judged and often lessens the intensity of the mother's responses. In addition, the kinesthetic movement of the car provides a soothing, lulling quality to the enclosed (womblike) space, perhaps, associatively, connecting to implicit memories of when the child would fall asleep in the car. In this more relaxed environment, like the younger child at bedtime, a time of diminished guardedness, processes of empathic attunement, and mutual recognition more easily flow.

Mother–Daughter Relationship in Illness and Old Age

The ongoing tie to the mother through different stages leads to a continual reorganizing of self and self-with-other schemas. Recurrent patterns of separation and loss and a reversal of a daughter's "mothering" a mother emerge in full force when a daughter faces caring for an ill or dying mother. By being thrust into the position of caring for her mother, the daughter may find an opportunity is created for resynthesizing her version of her mother's life, juxtaposed with the ambivalent feeling of moving into her mother's position in the life cycle. A clinical vignette illustrates a new relational experience for mother and daughter when the mother has lost her capacity to speak.

An analysand, Toni D., a single lawyer in her early fifties, was intimately involved in her mother's care at the end of her life. Her mother, a pathologically narcissistic woman, "used" Toni as an object to enhance her (mother's) specialness. In this longstanding relational pattern, Toni, viewed as flawed through her mother's eyes, like an "ugly duckling" was, nevertheless, expected to serve as her mother's caretaker. She felt devalued and denigrated, ultimately experiencing herself as undesirable and unlovable. Her mother, who experienced her physical beauty to be her most valued possession, suffered a stroke, and her body began to deteriorate. Toni, previously repulsed by her mother's touch, in response to her mother's loss of her ability to speak, began massaging her mother's body on her visits to the hospital. Poignantly and surprisingly, her mother, in a rare expression of genuine warmth and affection, began to hug Toni. In this mother–infant reversal, perhaps evoking the dual mother–infant identifications of each in the dyad, this self-centered, unempathic mother, reminiscent of the Wicked Queen in *Snow White* became the defanged, dying mother–baby. Her daughter, previously armored for the inevitable assault, for a brief time, was able to experience a new sense of agency in assuming a comforting motherly role. She soothed her mother by touch and, in turn, received her mother's hugs—an unexpected ending that was partially reparative of a poor beginning.

In like manner, the 1998 movie, *One True Thing* (Franklin), adapted from the autobiographically based novel by Anna Quindlen, portrays a mother–daughter relationship wherein the protagonist, Ellie Gulden, takes care of her mother, Kate, in the terminal phase of her life and comes to experience her mother fully and independently as a subject in her life. Through the central and often intertwined processes of increased empathic attunement and mutual recognition, Ellie matures by redefining her self and her relationship to her mother. I will describe this mother–daughter transformation in more detail.

Kate Gulden, Ellie's mother, has worked hard, by desire, at the seemingly effortless roles of wife and mother. George Gulden is the idealized, attractive, and adored father and husband, a successful academic who is writing the great American novel. Ellie, an Ivy League graduate, identified with her father and seeking his admiration, is ambitiously striving to become a successful journalist as she struggles with intimate relationships.

On Ellie's discovering Kate's advanced cancer, George tells Ellie that she will have to take a leave to care for her ill, stoic mother. Father evokes the mother–daughter unit, "Your mother cared for you when you were sick" (Franklin, 1998). When Ellie resists, reluctant to defer her aspirations, father turns on her with the "inescapable logic" of what it means to be a woman. "You have a Harvard education, but where is your heart?" (Franklin, 1998). The sudden reversal of the caregiver needing care, a major disturbance in this organized family system, creates a situation wherein the intellectual tie between father and daughter is disrupted. Biology is destiny when the father asserts that he is too important to leave his work and so Ellie must assume the caregiver's role.

Ellie laments, "One thing I never wanted to do was live my mother's life and there I was doing it" (Franklin, 1998). However, it is precisely this position that affords her an opportunity of understanding her mother as a subject in her life. Ellie's struggle to be in relation with and to differentiate from her mother, like that of many late adolescent girls, with her versions of her mother as both omnipotently perfect and disgustingly degraded, is condensed in her fear of becoming her mother. She recognizes her conscious adaptation to be one in which she is "remote and condescending."

We learn about Kate Gulden's life as Ellie enters it. Kate's social circle is a group of like-minded women, the Minis, who share their intimate lives and take on projects to beautify the town. Unlike the expansiveness of the professor father, "Mini" evokes associations of less than, Minnie Mouse, and ninny, all disparaged images, highlighting these women's willingness to be in the background. Ellie shudders at their lighthearted invitation to join their domestic, female world. She learns first hand, as she takes over her mother's household responsibilities, however, how much work is involved in keeping the home functioning well. While Kate, who may appear like the self-sacrificing mother, does it pleasurably, beautifully, and uncomplainingly, gaining recognition from these friends who notice each little touch, Ellie, in contrast, feels the lack of recognition and appreciation.

At the same time that her view of her mother is growing in complexity, Ellie is aware of a less idealized, more obviously narcissistic father. One scene juxtaposes the two images of Ellie—as-daughter-with-father and as-daughter–wife with father. Ellie is bursting with pride when her father asks her to write the introduction to his soon-to-be-published volume of essays, feeling recognized in her own right. Ellie's excitement is immediately followed by deflation as he then casually hands her two shirts to iron. George is being himself, as he has come to expect his wife to care for all of his needs. Ellie's profound disillusionment and anger with her father alternates with the new ways she takes in and appreciates her mother—her quiet strength, capacity to give to others, and subordination of her needs for the good of the family. Ellie's image of her adored father now shifts to that of a flawed man who refuses to put his own needs aside, as she becomes aware of his numerous affairs with graduate students, an attempt to support his fragile ego. Ellie realizes that she suppressed her subconscious knowledge of these events as a younger child.

In a final climactic scene between mother and daughter, we see Kate as a fully realized person, aware of all that goes on, having actively accepted her impending death. She is not "shushed" by her husband, her sense of propriety or her avoidance of the spotlight. She becomes, to Ellie, "an independent center, a recognized subject" who Ellie can take in as knowing and known, with awareness and depth. In her desire to die, Kate helps her daughter repair the rupture with her father and becomes the mother that Ellie needs.

KATE: He's going to need you, You're going to need each other. My god, you used to be so close. What happened? You two are so alike.

ELLIE: Please, don't say that.

KATE: Why? Because he's not perfect? Not the man you thought he was?

ELLIE: No, no I can't talk about this with you.

KATE: Come back here.

ELLIE: (murmurs) I can't. I can't.

KATE: Come here. I want to talk to you. Sit. Are you listening to me because I am only going to say this once and I probably shouldn't say it at all. There is nothing that you know about your father that I don't know. Nothing. And understand better. Okay? You make concessions when you're married a long time that you don't believe you'll make when you're beginning. When you're young, you say I'll never tolerate that, or this, or the other thing, but time goes by, darlin'. And you've slept together 1,000 nights, and you've smelled like spit up from his babies when they're sick and you've seen your body droop and get soft and sometimes you think" Oh, God! I'm not going to put up with it another minute!" but you wake up the next morning and the kitchen smells like coffee and the kids have their hair brushed all by themselves, and you look at your husband and, no, he's not the person you thought he was, but he's your life. And the kids and the house and everything is built around him. And that's your life. Your history too, and if you take him out that's like cutting his face out of all the pictures. It just makes a big hole and it ruins everything. You can be hard, Ellie, and you can be very judgmental, and with these two things I believe you're going to make a big mess out of your life, you wouldn't believe and I want to be able to tell you these things. When I think how most of the things you've learned came from your dad it just weakens my heart to think how little I've gotten done.

Ellie and Kate fight to speak.

KATE: I want to talk without you shushing me because what I say hurts you. I'm tired of being shushed. If I knew that you would be happy, I would close my eyes now, I would! It's so much easier to be happy, my love—to choose to love the things that you have. And you have so much! Instead of always yearning for what you are missing or what you are imagining you're missing. It's so much more peaceful.
(Franklin, 1998)

This sequence illustrates, in my view, a maturational step for mother and daughter. As Ellie revises and broadens her understanding of each parent and their relationship in the face of her mother's terminal illness, she is liberated from the constraints of the "identificatory love" (Benjamin, 1988) she has felt toward her father. This way of being has developed from the idealization of the father and the inability of the mother to be experienced as a woman in which "a feminine sense of desire and subjectivity in mutual relationship with a man come together" (Lichtenberg, 2002, p. 31). In the context of her impending death, Kate, attempting to restore the seemingly shattered relationship between father and daughter, uncharacteristically, refuses to be "shushed," and, from her point of view, risks hurting her daughter, by more fully and directly expressing herself. In fact, by this act of speaking her mind as a separate subject, Kate lifts the veil of her devalued femininity and subjectivity in the service of the idealization of the father and emerges as a mother who embodies wisdom, desire, and agency. In this scene, empathic attunement is in the background as mutual recognition (of separate subjectivities) between mother and daughter promote greater intimacy and respect.

Conclusion

I have attempted to illustrate, through the use of film and a clinical vignette, that the shifting equilibrium between two central avenues of relating, empathic attunement, and mutual recognition lead to growth and change in the mother–daughter relationship over one's lifetime. Empathic attunement facilitates the development and maintenance of a positive sense of self. Mutual recognition (Benjamin, 1988) or intersubjective relatedness (Stern, 1985) promotes the differentiation and appreciation of separate subjectivities. These pathways often have a background/foreground, complementary relationship to each other. Experience of empathic understanding and attunement can create a sufficiently positive cohesive sense of self, a sensibility for moving into a mode of mutual recognition, and greater differentiation and self-delineation. Difficulties arising when in the mode of mutual recognition often may be righted when one participant can shift into an empathic position, even temporarily.

Problematic interactions can occur in either pathway. Repetitive mismatches, that is, providing one form of relatedness when the mother or daughter is seeking greater responsiveness in the other pathway, at the moment, can thwart connection, and result in negative self and self-with-other percepts. The fluctuations and vicissitudes of these two paradigmatic modes of relating shed light on the lifelong mother–daughter relationship.

Acknowledgments

I wish to express my appreciation to the participants of the Roundtable Discussion Group for their constructive ideas. I particularly acknowledge Shelley Doctors, Ph.D., James Fosshage, Ph.D., Frank Lachmann, Ph.D., Joseph Lichtenberg, M.D., and Patricia Petrash, L.I.C.S.W. for their invaluable editorial suggestions.

REFERENCES

Balint, A. (1949), Love for the mother and mother–love, *Internat. J. Psycho-Anal.,* 30:251–259.

Balsam, R. (2000), The mother within the mother, *Psychoanal. Quart.,* 89:145–159.

Beebe, B. & Lachmann, F. (2002), *Infant Research and Adult Treatment.* Hillsdale, NJ: Analytic Press.

Benjamin, J. (1988), *The Bonds of Love.* New York: Pantheon.

_____ (2004), Beyond doer and done to: An intersubjective view of thirdness, *Psychoanal. Quart.,* 73:5–46.

Bernstein, D. (1983), The female superego: A different perspective, *Internat. J. Psycho-Anal.,* 64:187–201.

Bernstein, P. (2005), Mothers and daughters from today's psychoanalytic perspective, *Psychoanal. Inq.,* 24:601–628.

Bucci, W. (2002), The referential process, consciousness, and the sense of self, *Psychoanal. Inq.,* 22:766–793.

Chodorow, N. (1978), *The Reproduction of Mothering: Psychoanalysis and the Sociology of Gender.* Berkeley: University of California Press.

Davis, M. and Walbridge, D. (1981). *Boundry and Space: An Introduction to the work of D. W. Winnicott.* London: H. Karnac Ltd.

Fosshage, J. (1997), Listening/experiencing perspectives and the quest for a facilitative responsiveness. In: *Conversations in Self Psychology,* ed. A. Goldberg. Hillsdale, NJ: The Analytic Press 13:33–55.

Franklin, C. (Director) (1998). *One true thing.* [Motion picture] United States: Universal Studios.

Kohut, H. (1959), Introspection, empathy and psychoanalysis, *J. Amer. Psychoanal. Assn.,* 7: 459–483.

_____ (1971), *The Analysis of the Self.* New York: International Universities Press.

_____ (1977), *The Restoration of the Self.* New York: International Universities Press.

_____ (1984), *How Does Analysis Cure?* Chicago, IL: University of Chicago Press.

Lachmann, F. (1986), Interpretation of psychic conflict and adversarial relationships, *Psychoanal. Psychol.,* 3:341–355.
_____ (2004), On the co-construction of empathy. Presented to the Eastern Regional Division of the International Council of Self Psychology, Washington, D.C.
Lichtenberg, J. (2002), Intimacy with the gendered self, *Selbstpsychologie,* 7:40–60.
Nahum, J. P. (1994), New theoretical vistas in psychoanalysis: Louis Sander's theory of early development, *Psychoanal. Psychol.,* 11:1–19.
Rodgers, M. (1972), *Freaky Friday.* New York: Harper Collins.
Sander, L. Stechler, G., Burns, P., & Lee, A. (1979). Change in infant and caregiver variables over the first two months of life: Integration of action in early development. In: *Origins of the Infant's Social Responsiveness,* ed. E. Thoman. Hillsdale, NJ: Lawrence Erlbaum Associates, Inc., pp. 349–407.
Stern, D. N. (1995), *The Motherhood Constellation.* New York: Basic Books.
_____ (1985), *The Interpersonal World of the Infant.* New York: Basic Books.
Waters, M. (Director) (2003) *Freaky Friday.* [Motion picture] United States: Walt Disney.
Winnicott, D. W. (1956), Primary maternal preoccupation. In: *Collected Papers: Through Paediatrics to Psycho-analysis.* New York: Basic Books, 1958.
_____ (1962), Providing for the child in health and crisis. In: *The Maturational Processes and the Facilitating Environment.* New York: International Universities Press, 1965.
_____ (1965), The capacity to be alone. In: The Maturational Processes and the Facilitating Environment. New York: International Universities Press, 1965.
_____ (1966), The ordinary devoted mother. In: *Babies and Their Mothers.* U.S.: Addison-Wesley, 1987.
_____ (1971), *Playing and Reality.* New York: Routledge.
Wolf, E. (1988), *Treating the Self.* New York: Guilford Press.
_____ (1980), On the developmental line of self-object relations. In: *Advances in Self Psychology,* ed. A. Goldberg. New York: International Universities Press, pp. 117–130.

6317 Kenhowe Drive
Bethesda, MD 20817
hershbs@erols.com

Searching for Togetherness: The Simultaneous Treatment of a Mother and Her Early Adolescent Daughter

SARALEA E. CHAZAN, PH.D.

Simultaneous treatment involves the separate treatment of parent and child by the same therapist. In this supportive–expressive psychotherapy, the focus of treatment is on the connecting points in the relationship between parent and child that cause each member of the dyad to experience difficulties ranging from enmeshment to alienation. The context provided by the parent–child relationship provides a background for the actual, as well as the potential, identities of each of its members. While transforming elements of this relationship radiate change outward, affecting the larger family unit, facets of the parent–child relationship also affect the inner subjective experience and personality structure of each participant. What characterizes this treatment method is not only external arrangements but also the complex nature of the developing transference–countertransference relationships. The therapist is the nodal point, integrating levels of reality by experiencing and communicating new understandings to each member of the dyad.

THE NECESSITY TO INTERVENE AT THE LEVEL OF THE PARENT–CHILD relationship has consistently been the focus of child therapists. Depending on the theoretical perspective, the cultural climate, and the pragmatics of practicality, different paradigms of treatment have been used. Melitta Sperling (1950, 1951, 1954, 1970, 1982) described her approach to the simultaneous treatment of parent and child as providing opportunities for

Saralea E. Chazan, Ph.D., is a faculty member of the Institute Child, Adolescent and Family Psychotherapy (ICAFS).

the observation of the child's ego and the superego development within the context of the parent–child relationship. She described simultaneous treatment as facilitating the detection of parental attitudes toward instinctual control, separation from the child, and changes in dependency. Therefore, according to Sperling, an approach based on psychoanalytic insight, confronting the parent with her unconscious conflicts concerning her child, was often the most effective mode of treatment, providing an additional gain of prevention of future difficulties, as well as providing the best remedy for the difficulties at hand. The early analysts, including Dorothy Burlingham (1951, 1955), Anna Freud (1950), Ilse Hellman (1960, 1990), and others (Kolansky and Moore, 1966; Levy 1960; Chethik, 1976; Shapiro, Fraiberg, and Adelson 1980; Sholevar, et al., 1989) agreed on the need for alteration of treatment parameters as a means to an end, that is, as a way to deal with the unconscious resistance of the enmeshed dyad.

More recently, there has been an upsurge in interest in working with parents both here in the United States and in England. For example, Jack and Kelly Novick (2001, 2002a, b, c) focus on the unfolding of parent work that corresponds with each phase of child treatment. They state that a central goal of child analysis is movement out of closed system functioning between parent and child to a more open system of self-regulation between the parents and child. Viviane Green (2000) describes the importance of constructing a therapeutic space that allows for and encourages recreation of the child in the mind of the parents. She emphasizes the need for a strong feeling of safety in the relationship between parents and their child's therapist. This safe feeling enables the parents to begin a process of identification with and internalization of the therapist. It is through this integrative process that parents are then able to initiate their own capacity for reflection about their child.

A concise summary of some of the aspects shared by these newer approaches to parents and children in treatment can be found in the comments of Neil Altman (2000). From the perspective of attachment theory, he brings together several examples that demonstrate how the child is induced to behave in a way that validates the projections of the parents. Within this context, he emphasizes the therapist's capacity to "play" with the parent's projections, to accept them while not being bound to them unreflectively, as carrying the potential for therapeutic leverage. The reader is also directed to other recent articles pertaining to this topic, including publications by Altman, et al. (2002); Bartram (2003); Edwards and Maltby (1998); Klauber (1991); Lassonde and Mayes (2005); Rustin (1999); and Arietta Slade (1999).

Margaret Mahler expressed concern that, if the same therapist saw both parent and child, a double transference–countertransference problem might arise. In her tripartite model, the parents and young child were seen together, and the parents were seen separately for their individual treatment (Kohn, 1976). This treatment model was extended by Eleanor Galenson in her work with young children (e.g., Galenson and Fields, 1989; Galenson, 1991). Conversely, Peter Buirski and Cathy Buirski (1980) wrote about the risks of a split transference that might occur when two therapists treated members of the same family. A useful summary of the early literature on this topic appears in an article by Ben Kohn (1976), in which the author reflects on the technical problems arising when both parent and child are seen by the same therapist.

This brief overview is offered as background for my emerging interest in simultaneous treatment. Over the past 20 years, I have found it to be an intriguing and productive approach for some of my parents and their children. Although wary at first to proceed into what I perceived to be hazardous territory, with the support of two of my mentors, I continued to explore this paradigm. As a result of these efforts, I published a conceptual formulation and several cases in a volume titled *Simultaneous Treatment of Parent and Child* (2003). It is focused on the dyadic issues that impinge on the adaptive development of parent and child. Given specific patients and specific life circumstances, it can be the optimal treatment choice. In some instances, as in the example described in this article, simultaneous treatment may be appropriate for a portion of the treatment that later proceeds on an individual basis. Simultaneous treatment is a treatment modality based on psychoanalytic understanding that is targeted at parent–child relationships. For a more detailed survey of the literature and a procedural description of the treatment process, I refer the reader to my book, cited earlier.

Clearly, simultaneous treatment places many demands on its participants. The parent needs to be firmly allied with the goals of treatment. It is not a treatment geared to individual problems; rather, the relationship bond between parent and child is the subject of the treatment and the object to receive treatment. Not all parent–child dyads are candidates for this type of intervention. On one level, boundaries are clear, with confidentiality for both parent and child; however, on another level, the very essence of the treatment involves boundary seeking and boundary setting. The therapist, as participant in and observer of the subjective worlds of both parent and child, can foster new common ground in the parent–child relationship through enhanced processes of recognition, reciprocity, and mutuality.

Conflictual issues focused on feelings of rivalry and competition are better understood and coped with when given a meaningful background of shared emotional experience.

Therapists working in simultaneous treatment need to be versed in both child and adult therapy. This is not a treatment modality for the novice. In addition, these therapists must have the capacity to tolerate ambiguity and have a welcoming attitude toward points of view other than their own. Working with the parent–child dyad is to come to grips with understanding experience as complex and multidetermined. If the therapist is overinvested for personal reasons in any one perspective, she will be unable to appreciate the complexity of her position as a participant–observer and will be ineffective in her therapeutic interventions. The therapist's own therapy is a valuable source of insight. The integration of personal and professional knowledge is essential for maintaining both therapeutic understanding and endurance.

The nature of the transference–countertransference relationship in simultaneous treatment has many different aspects. The therapist's position in both treatments is linked, as well as separate; it has immediate impact in the present moment and resonates with past generations. The therapist travels to and fro between child and parent, relating to each separately, thereby suggesting the possibility of new movement and change not only within the separate therapeutic relationships, but within the parent–child relationship, as well. This statement does not mean that the therapist shares information, acting as a carrier between parent and child. Rather, it is the mental and physical activity of the therapist, who can clearly hold in mind and reflect about each of her patients, that implies possibilities for new openness between parent and child.

Although the therapist is in intimate contact with each patient, boundaries of confidentiality are carefully maintained. The relationships are not symmetrical, because they are based on the understanding of generational difference; the child is the younger patient, the parent is an adult. For the parent, a degree of altruism is required. Simultaneous treatment is not a complete individual treatment; it is a treatment focused on improvement of the parent–child relationship. Therefore, the parent, in assuming the parental role, puts aside exploration of personal goals that do not contribute toward the shared goal of an improved parent–child relationship. In the mother–daughter pair described in this article, the impact of divorce, role reversals, and entanglements with extended family members resulted in a confusion of loyalties, empowerment, and responsibilities. Simultaneous treatment focused on the confusions and unclear boundaries that influenced, in a pervasive way, the understanding of gender and the role of sexuality.

The reader's attention is directed to the fact that this approach to treatment is not gender specific. Although most commonly the parent involved is the mother, it could be the father, grandparent, or guardian on whom the child is dependent, who brings the child to treatment. Similarly, in the author's experience, the child patient could be a boy or girl. In this article, we will be focusing, however, on the unique features of treatment when the patient is an early adolescent girl accompanied by her mother and when the gender-specific features of their relationship impinge on the treatment process. Simultaneous treatment appears especially applicable to those mother–daughter dyads in which boundary issues, both gender and intergenerational, have become deeply laden with conflict (Lane and Chazan, 1988). Mother and daughter both come to use the therapist as a third party, with intimate links to each of them.

In sum, simultaneous treatment is not a complete individual treatment, rather, it is an intervention focused on the dyadic relationship itself and, as such, enables the participants to process emotions not otherwise approachable. Simultaneous treatment enables the dyad to sustain the tensions between them, allowing them to recognize and experience similarities and differences in relationship from newly perceived nonthreatening perspectives. These new contours and configurations in relationship patterns can then be used constructively toward creative ends.

Susanna: A Young Girl in Crisis From Within and Without

Susanna was 12 and a half years old at the time she was referred to me for treatment by her pediatrician. She was an only child, living with her mother; her parents had separated a year previous to our meeting, after a marriage of 15 years. Her parents informed her the impending separation would occur after the Thanksgiving holiday. However, Mr. S. remained in the home until after Christmas at Susanna's request. Susanna feared she "might be going crazy." She was afraid of "growing up bad" and developed a recurrent desire to "make love to a woman."

With her father, Susanna became increasingly fearful and especially afraid of staying overnight at his apartment. She began incessantly posing questions to her mother about the couple's sexual behavior, for instance, "did they make love the evening before he left." Mrs. S. was not sure how to answer her daughter's questions. She was alarmed by Susanna's recurrent intrusive thoughts and feelings of depression that included suicidal ideation. She was asking the therapist for assistance with her daughter and her own feelings of being overwhelmed by confusion and anxiety.

Relevant Family and Developmental History

Susanna's parents were both from families with strong ethnic and religious bonds. They had met while still in high school and were married several years after graduation. Mr. S., in his mid-thirties, was strikingly handsome and tall, with dark hair and an extremely intense manner. He was employed as a computer analyst. Mrs. S., also in her mid-thirties, in contrast was a short, appealing looking person with a calm, organized manner. She was employed as an inventory specialist, having begun full-time work when Susanna was five years old. Child care was provided by various extended family members, primarily the paternal grandmother.

Susanna's extended family all lived in very close proximity to one another. Mr. S's younger sister resided in the same apartment building with her husband and two children, both considerably younger than Susanna. The paternal grandmother was described as overprotective and domineering. Her husband died when Susanna was seven years old. His death followed a long period of illness. This was one of a series of losses that would greatly affect Susanna. The dominant figure in the family clan was Nannie, Susanna's paternal great grandmother. She died when Susanna was nine years old after suffering a long period of illness and repeated hospitalizations. Mrs. S. described Nannie as a remarkable person, resilient and capable. She featured prominently in Susanna's early years as a caregiver, someone reliable and loyal on whom Mrs. S could rely. This positive memory provided a beneficent expectation for therapeutic intervention. Mrs. S. felt Nannie's loss to be extremely painful but found herself unable to grieve. Similarly, as subsequently revealed in treatment, this unrelenting sense of loss was a major factor in Susanna's sexualized lesbian longings. Although several relatives lived in close proximity to Suzanna's home, none could fill the void resulting from Nannie's death.

Mrs. S.'s family of origin also lived close by. Her mother and younger unmarried sister lived together. The maternal grandfather died suddenly when Susanna was four years old. His loss was felt deeply as he was a source of nurturance and warmth for the family. Mrs. S's mother was described as intolerant and volatile. After the death of the maternal grandfather, Mrs. S., the more capable of the two sisters, became the mediator responsible for settling arguments within the family. On first meeting with Susanna, the family names were very confusing to me. Susanna, her mother, and her mother's unwed sister, all shared names beginning with the same letter. This similarity appeared to obscure generational and age differences between the three women. The younger sister was employed as a nurse; she had never developed an interest in dating men or in having her own family.

Susanna was a planned child, born after two years of marriage. Although the pregnancy was normal, birth was by emergency Caesarean section. The umbilicus had been wrapped around the baby's neck, and labor lasted fifteen hours. Susanna's early development proceeded along expected milestones. Because of the circumstances surrounding her birth and being the first child and grandchild, her early months were accompanied by a combination of special attention, parental anxiety, and worry. Both parents recalled Susanna as having colic as an infant. Until three months of age she needed to be held "constantly." Susanna slept in her parents' bedroom the first year of her life. She was bottle fed and weaned at approximately sixteen months. Five months after the birth of Susanna, Mrs. S. experienced a life-threatening tubular pregnancy and suffered from pervasive fears of becoming pregnant again. These fears led to a decision to have her tubes permanently tied. Thus, as Mrs. S. later confided, maternity came to be associated for her with threatening feelings of fear, anxiety, and inadequacy. Nannie cared for Susanna during Mrs. S's ten days in the hospital. Reportedly, Susanna continued to thrive despite the separation, recognized her mother on her return, and did not cry a lot. Subsequently, Mrs. S. changed this narrative. She related that no one else sensed a change in Susanna, but that nonetheless she subsequently felt Susanna turned away from her and tended to prefer others. Mrs. S. expressed that in retrospect Susanna's negativity combined with her own apprehensions had deleterious effects on the ensuing development of the mother–daughter attachment. An additional component of wariness and insecurity had been added to a relationship already marked by anxious concern. Not only was Mrs. S. concerned about being able to parent and sustaining the survival of her infant child; at this juncture, becoming a parent became associated with anxiety about her own survival as well. Reportedly, Mr. S. was not supportive of his wife and maintained both emotional distance and frequent absences from the home on business trips subsequent to her return.

Mrs. S. reported that as a young child Susanna was often oppositional. A frequent issue between them was intense anger with her mother for leaving her in the care of others. Her oppositional behavior at these times was distinctly different from her usual more "good little girl" stance and her desire to be like her mother and remain consistently calm. According to both parents, Susanna did not develop an ambivalent attitude toward her father. The father–daughter relationship consistently remained distant and aloof, a somewhat shadowy relationship, relatively less defined, more prone to ambiguity and misunderstanding by both parties.

Despite her mother's description of Susanna's latency years as a relatively somnolent period, with Susanna a compliant and well-behaved child, from Susanna's perspective it was not calm. These years were marked in her memory as filled with loneliness and isolation. She recounted missing the company of her parents, particularly the absence of her mother. During treatment, the return of repressed memories revealed her to have been sexually vulnerable, first to the overtures of her girlfriend and then to the inappropriate "playful" sexual advances proffered by her paternal uncle. Susanna was looking for affection and welcomed the warmth of these relations but lived in fear of their eventual revelation and the aspects of herself these behaviors would imply. Another family secret was in the process of evolution during these years, with Susanna as the "bad girl" protagonist. If this "bad girl" with sexual desires were to be revealed on center stage, Susanna's worst fears would become realized.

Within the context of treatment, definite corroboration was given for Susanna's perception of strained family relations and a home life that stifled emotional expression. Susanna's friendships focused on her paternal aunt and her girlfriend. Most of her experience was triangular, with Susanna either in the role of voyeur or as the passive recipient of aggressive or sexual overtures. As discussed earlier, this passivity later proved to be a cover for unconscious strivings that became activated in fantasies in which Susanna perceived herself to be the active pursuer (Blos, 1962). Taking the assertive, more sexualized position could be understood in part as Susanna's efforts to differentiate herself from earlier pervasive passive longings to be cared for (Fast, 1984). Dreams became a frequent avenue to reach highly sexualized feelings, suggesting the presence of primal scene material and perhaps inappropriate exposure. Overt sexual overtures or behaviors were denied by each parent. However, unclear boundaries were substantiated in sleeping arrangements. Mrs. S. frequently vacated her bedroom, leaving Susanna who had awakened with fearful thoughts to sleep with her father. Later in treatment, Susanna revealed that she often imagined herself to be hidden away as a small kitten in her parents' closet observing their sexual behaviors.

Puberty began for Susanna at 11 years of age with the appearance of pubic hair; menses arriving at age 11 and a half years. There was no apparent physical discomfort with these developments; however, Susanna's outward appearance began to change radically. She dressed in a sexy, stylish manner, appearing older than her age. She dyed her hair platinum and demanded new clothes. Clearly, many changes were occurring, as expressed through these new accoutrements. Susanna's image of herself was undergoing rapid change. Her appearance became a sharp contrast to her mother's conservative style. Susanna began experiencing difficulties with her friends. She alternatively felt persecuted and then loved by them. This fluctuation in attitude was accompanied by rapid shifts in mood, varying from sadness, to preoccupation with appearance, to occasional periods of fearfulness. Her alliances would change daily. Parental separation furthered Susanna's already shaky sense of generalized insecurity, increasing feelings of hostility, as well as perceived dangers.

Initial Meeting with Susanna

At our first meeting, I encountered a tall, lithe, likable young person. Although her pain was evident in general tension and anxiety, she readily engaged in conversation, conveying her sadness and anxiety in occasional quiet bursts of tears. Susanna had brown eyes and light brown straight hair, and she dressed in modish, sophisticated attire, making her appear more mature than her chronological age. Her main discomfort was anxiety associated with recurring thoughts about being a lesbian, because of her almost constant desire to make love to a woman and the fears these hidden feelings evoked. Susanna did not specify a specific woman she desired, but remembered the excitement of engaging in sexual play with her girlfriend and said she felt excited and attracted to women she encountered in casual relationships. Additional complaints included general dysphoria, characterized by feeling down in the dumps, hopeless, irritable, insomnia, fatigue, feelings of worthlessness and inappropriate guilt, diminished ability to concentrate, and recurrent thoughts of death and suicide. These symptoms meet the criteria for Major Depressive Episode (American Psychiatric Association, 2000). Susanna was open about recounting her experiences and readily told me why she associated these feelings chronologically with the upheaval caused by her parents' divorce. She was receptive to the suggestion of psychotherapy and optimistic that treatment would alleviate her distress.

Initial Meeting with Mrs. S.

Mrs. S. was shocked by the discovery of her husband's betrayal. Although the couple decided to separate, they agreed with Susanna's request that Mr. S. would remain in the home until after Christmas. In hindsight, Mrs. S. felt this might have been confusing to Susanna, as husband and wife continued to share the same bed. Parental actions at this decisive point were clearly being dictated by Susanna. Collusion with Susanna's wishes was enacted in this decision to masquerade that the parental relationship was still intact. Secretiveness had a long tradition in Susanna's extended family as a means of coping with shameful, unacceptable life events and emotions. Both parents agreed to empower their child to decide how and when the separation would be revealed.

Mrs. S. was confused and alarmed by her daughter's dilemma. Susanna's strong desire to make love to a woman made no sense to Mrs. S. She was aware of no precedents for these feelings and described her daughter as having grown up the beloved, somewhat spoiled child, first grandchild of a close family with strong religious beliefs. Mrs. S. expressed heightened anxiety as she recounted feeling helpless, not knowing how to respond to her daughter's questions and worries. She herself worried that perhaps something terrible was happening to her daughter that was irreversible. In a composed, yet exaggerated hysterical style, she viewed Susanna's homosexual fears as totally beyond comprehension. Mrs. S. asked if I might work with her as well, alongside my work with her daughter, so they might regain a sense of balance and shared understanding.

Treatment Plan

A plan evolved for the therapist to meet separately with mother and daughter once a week. Within a month, Susanna's sessions had increased to twice weekly, while Mrs. S. retained once a week separate meetings with the therapist for eighteen months. The dyadic relationship of mother and daughter was the central focus of treatment. Subsequent to this period of treatment of the mother–daughter relationship (twice-weekly sessions for the child, weekly sessions for the mother), infrequent contacts with Mrs. S. occurred, often by phone. These contacts had the focus of supportive parent counseling, beacuse Mrs. S. was moving forward with her life and felt her personal issues had been alleviated. During the period of simultaneous treatment, Mr. S. participated at infrequent intervals, always at the request and in the presence of Mrs. S. His tone could be questioning, curious, and, though at times skeptical, was generally receptive. Susanna maintained her twice-weekly individual sessions throughout high school and college, traveling a distance to the therapist's office after relocation of the family. The ensuing treatment with Susanna followed the paradigm of individual psychoanalytically oriented psychotherapy, enriched by the background of the prior experience with simultaneous treatment.

This article will not attempt an overview of the treatment process. Rather, some selected aspects of the eighteen months of simultaneous treatment will be summarized, with special focus on a single session that gives poignant expression to many of Susanna's experiences in a condensed manner.

Aspects of Susanna's First Year of Treatment

As we shared the experience of being together, Susanna's fears of being a lesbian gradually subsided. She felt comfort in expressing her feelings of loneliness and longings to be close with a woman who would care for her and help her to understand the many physical sensations that accompanied puberty. She wondered if she had always linked these desires for intimacy with the sexual actions of touching and sensuous arousal.

When she described the sexual play with her friend, she focused on the activities of touching and being touched; sucking and being sucked in by the other. These associations led to the increasingly dominant themes of loneliness and longings for Nannie with whom she found comfort. Susanna recalled snuggling up against Nannie's warm body when she was a young child. I reflected with her about how a very young child would desire to suck and take in the source of this warmth and comfort. The recollection of these early feelings deepened our therapeutic relationship. Susanna felt secure and safe in these moments of being together; the fears of being overwhelmed by excitement and acting out her feelings diminished. As suggested by one of the reader's of this article, Susanna could gradually begin to separate emotionally from her family without resorting to feelings of shame to gain a sense of autonomy.

Susanna's deepest anxieties resonated with her fear of being different—so different from others that she would be rejected by them. Choosing to act on her desire for sexual closeness with a woman would validate her worst fears of differentness and mark her forever as a castoff, someone not worthy of her family's love. Susanna's initial presentation of brazen sexuality concealed a more global driven state to connect and be recognized as a maturing young woman, particularly by other women. She took comfort in the stability and acceptance she found in the therapeutic relationship. Negativity experienced by her mother appeared infrequently in our relationship when she would protest that I would be critical of her behavior or find her wishes unacceptable. Although she found solace in the understanding that her desires were ubiquitous, she would not relinquish her anger at having been misunderstood and pushed aside by her parents. Susanna expressed her resentment directly to her mother, sharply critical of her mother's failure to provide safe care.

Rather than remaining focused on victimization, she reviewed a history of personal losses and how they had overwhelmed her family. Indeed, loss was the dominant feature of her past intimate relationships. Susanna gave me a large picture of a girl, sitting alone and looking wistfully into the distance. The image was drawn in black ink; background surroundings were rendered in black-and-white geometric patterns. Susanna indicated she had drawn this picture several years before our meeting, copying it from a picture she had seen. The qualities of absence of life and controlled execution of detail were predominant in this painstaking exact reproduction of a young girl.

Although Mr. S. was a distant parent, nonetheless, Susanna ruminated about him, bringing him alive in her personal world. He combined scary and risky attributes of the desired male parent. Thus she desired not only women, but men as well, revealing a more fundamental undifferentiated orientation toward gender and sexuality. As part of this fluctuating and confusing sense of herself, Susanna at times imagined herself as a son, rather than a daughter. She was convinced her mother's second pregnancy (terminated early) was a boy child. Perhaps in this masculine body she would be special to her father. Then, as her envy subsided, she recalled her maternal grandfather who was loving and caring. I felt that at these moments Susanna had begun the process of acknowledgement of what she had lost and had begun to mourn a treasured personal relationship. Interestingly, the key to this process of reworking was a male, the maternal grandfather, equally beloved by her mother as well. Clearly, at this point in treatment she was able to use the security of the transference relationship to explore varied fantasies of herself and share diverse renditions of her personal identity with me. I felt a corresponding sense of relief from tension and happiness as Susanna made use of her newly acquired emotional freedom.

Ambivalence and fluctuation of affect states toward herself and others followed in rapid succession in her reverie. Gradually, over the course of simultaneous treatment, Susanna began to sustain a more consistently trusting attitude toward her mother. Anxieties and fears were challenging as she began to contrast her experiences of being the same, and yet different, in relationship to her mother and to myself. Changes in the mother–daughter relationship were fundamental to Susanna's growing acquisition of the capacity to relate to peers as well.

Basic to this therapeutic process was the adaptation to difference. Susanna began to reflect on the difference between her desires and the actuality of her life. The sense of disappointment was great; the wishes to be a boy, to completely possess a woman, to have her parents together, to have loved ones return again were recurrent pervasive themes. Susanna struggled to modify her fantasy of being able to have all of her needs and desires met, a defense against her overwhelming sense of loss and rejection. Although she wished for sameness, this wish was also threatening as it eclipsed the expression of her individuality. (For further discussion of these issues see J. Benjamin (1995), also P. Blos (1980) for relevance to adolescent development.)

Brief Selections from a Session with Susanna at the Close of One Year of Treatment

The evening before this session, Susanna attended a birthday party for her father, held by her paternal grandmother in her home. Susanna and her grandmother were joined by her father's sister family. Susanna had baked a cake for her father, and her aunt was going to take part of the cake home. Although Susanna insisted on also getting part of that remaining piece, she was furious.

> He said, "I can't take the whole cake home." I was like ... try ... try ... try really hard. ... I mean if I gave him another present, was she going

> to take half of it … now, come on. … I guess I gave him a present he could share and he wanted to share part of it.

Susanna continued to voice her grievances against her aunt, who—she felt—might also horn in on an invitation to a show she wanted to see with her father. Later, she relented and said this probably won't happen because her father, being a practical guy, would not take her to a show; rather her mother would probably offer to take her. She went on to be further critical of her aunt, disapproving of her lazy and indulgent lifestyle. Susanna elaborated on how she had managed negotiating tasks with her mother so she would agree to type her homework. Mother now would not impose her standards of cleanliness on her and she could keep her room in a way comfortable for herself. But, then, she suggested I would probably disapprove.

Susanna has given voice to her inner wishes for exclusivity with her father, where she would possess him totally, leaving nothing to share with her rival. She then relents, commenting on how she had been the one to gift him with nurturance that could be shared. Similarly, her mother is perceived as recognizing her needs, while in contrast I am the one who is critical. Perhaps, I add, it is also I who offer her only half a cake by extending therapy to include her mother.

Susanna recalled a dream she had before the birthday party for her father. Her mother had told me of her concern when her daughter awakened with a nightmare. Susanna told her mother she would share it with me.

> It scared me. It was my grandmother and grandfather. He's dead—he's been dead at least 8 years. He died when I was young. I just don't know what ever made me think of him. They weren't allowed to see—they had another grandchild and they weren't able to see him. So, I had to seek him out for them to get to him … to take away with them, wherever they were going.
>
> … It just scared me. I thought why did I think of him (not clear grandfather, or child) after all these years. … They were driving away. Did you ever see the movie "Grease" … at the end they drive away into the sky. That's what it reminded me of, when they drive away … my grandparents. It was weird. … There's only one other grandchild, a boy, the same age I am, 5 years old. I think I got him from my grandmother's house … it was very dark inside … it scared me.
>
> … I was pretty close I guess to my grandfather. From what I remember he was like, a baker, and he made pies. I can remember help-

> ing him to make pies … like little tarts and stuff like that. I think I was closer to him than to my grandmother … I'm not so sure about that. … Yeah … I remember he would take half of the dough and put it in the cabinet. I could never figure out when I was little why he would do something like that.
>
> He would take half and put it in the cabinet to rise, or something like that, when he was making the pie. I could never … I was always so fascinated with his taking the dishes out of the cabinet and everything. Why was he doing this … you know?

I resonated to Susanna's curiosity about seeing her grandfather put half of the cake away. I also pointed out to her how she had the dream about her grandfather the baker, and then, she had baked a cake as a present for her father's birthday. I further suggested grandfather's pies were made with love … he was making good things and yet he put half away. She laughed as she thought about this, and I suggested it was almost as if there was another child there, who you were saving half for "a secret" a hidden part. I asked if that idea scared her.

> No … Like my mom, she told me at one time she was carrying a baby and she lost him. … But for some reason, I always thought it was a boy. I don't know … and the name Adam always came to mind. … I don't know. I always assumed it was a boy. … I always wanted a little brother. … I guess I felt deprived when I was younger … I was never very talented at anything … never had a brother or sister … and then, my parents got divorced. Probably I wouldn't have to go to a babysitter or have a brother or sister to go with ….
>
> He just … it just scared me because I said "Oh, here he is in my dream!" It was like he came back to haunt me.

The session continued with more memories associated with loss and loneliness, beginning with the recent death of her cat, then returning to the loss of her father's father whose death she had not understood, to the prior death, when she was a toddler, of her mother's father. She had an early memory of going to the hospital with her mother to collect his belongings. She used the verb carrying three times to describe how mother was carrying her in her arms. Susanna recalls her mother's many tears and sadness: "… I was so young … my mother was bouncing me down the hall on the side of her hip." She recalled her confusion over her maternal grandfather's death.

"I asked where he was, because everybody else was there. My mother said he was sleeping, or something like that, only he wouldn't come out. ... I couldn't understand all the sadness, and yet they had a party. ... I just kept looking for him."

Susanna continued with the story of Nannie's death and recounted how close they had been and how much she missed her. She recalled her father as not being available at these events, it was her mother who carried all the responsibility and work. She told of a fantasy friend she had named Jason. Laughingly she recounted she thought of him "just" as a friend, not a boyfriend. Susanna went on to tell again of her mother's loss of a child and how she felt her mother would certainly have wished for more children. She felt it still hurt her mother to talk about it.

> Though she is happy with me. ... When I was born I was like gold to both sides of the family. The first grandchild on both sides. Now there are two more—silver and bronze—(laughs) ... you know, we all could be made of the same metal.

The session highlights Susanna's early experience of multiple losses condensed in the early perception of hidden, unshared aspects of the self. Rather then being a partner in the playful give and take, back and forth of early social experience, Susanna feels herself to have been deprived of half her share. She remains held by her mother in an embrace that allows movement only when child and mother are one unit. Susanna is denied the opportunities to ambulate away from and reconnoiter with her mother. Still restrained in this early holding position, magnified by extended family relationships, she remains alive only as an extension of her mother's body. This failure to differentiate self from other results in deep longings to remain in the arms of her mother, rather than sharing in the reciprocal experiences of leaving and being left. Susanna depicted in this session how she entered treatment with the overwhelming wish/fear of possessing all of her mother and of possessing a hidden fantasy sibling, or friend, who would offer both mother and daughter the illusion of completeness.

Summary of Mrs. S's Simultaneous Treatment

During the first year of treatment, Mrs. S. felt her therapy to be an essential part of her postseparation recovery. In the following six-month period, she came to view treatment as self-enhancing and a way she could freely express and explore her feelings about new relationships. Perhaps because of the traumatic magnitude of these challenges, she redoubled her efforts to help her daughter in every way possible. In part, I was perceived by Mrs. S. as a repair person, someone who could assist her to recuperate and mend her injuries. However, she also viewed me as invasive and placed a distance between us by focusing on Susanna's feelings and only later making reference to herself. Using her motherhood in this way could be viewed as having a defensive edge. From another perspective, it could be viewed as a necessary prelude to confronting her own feelings. This pattern was also observed in the initial recounting of developmental history. It appeared a necessary process to at first view me as helpful to her child, before she turned the lens to focus on her personal concerns.

Mrs. S. was perplexed and more than a bit dismayed at Susanna's verbalized homoerotic desires. She, herself, had always shared confidences with her younger sister, and they remained very close. Her ties to her own mother were more distant, as she perceived her to be demanding and critical. Mrs. S. did not repeat these difficulties with me; instead, it was often my role to soften her judgments of Susanna and provide the balm of new understanding or a different point of view. Therapy became a time when Mrs. S. could voice her intense anger and shame without the fear of experiencing humiliation or harsh judgment.

Mrs. S. worked hard to gain professional status and to support her daughter and herself. She was intensely resentful of her husband for not being a better provider. Although hostile toward him, she tried to avoid burdening her daughter with her bereft and angry feelings. Therapy provided her with an opportunity to vent these negative feelings that she would rationalize at first were because of her daughter's demands. With further exploration, it became clear her resentment was more deeply based. Mrs. S. resented not only the betrayal of her husband, but also the loss of her father that left her at the head of the nuclear family. Her mother and sister, both dependent on her, placed many demands on her. She had been an excellent student, but did not go to college and instead went to work so she could provide needed income. After her marriage, she continued working and perceived herself as searching for fulfillment in the role of the "good little wife."

About three months into treatment, Mrs. S. began to pursue a formal ending to her marital relationship through a legal divorce. Taking this step on her own initiative toward final termination of her marriage appeared to free Mrs. S. from inhibitions about sharing confidences about the marital relationship. This intimate reflection would have felt initially to be embarrassing and somehow disloyal, not only to her estranged husband, but to his family as well. As in all other aspects of this enmeshed family, these reflections about herself and her husband were complex—full of secretiveness and intrigue. Mrs. S. had been married 10 years when her husband revealed to her the events surrounding his father's death. Because of his father's long illness and addiction after amputation of his leg, a war injury, Mr. S. often served as his father's nurse. His mother toiled with daily routines, taking menial jobs to augment family income. Only immediate family members knew of this situation; neighbors were never aware of the family's burden. Mr. S. became devoted to his father's care; when he died, Mr. S. tried to deny the extent of his personal loss. According to Mrs. S., her husband looked up to his father and placed him on a pedestal, admiring him for his strength in the ordeal. Gradually, Mrs. S. began to share more details about the couple's most intimate moments. She felt she was always the pursuer, initiating sexual relationships. At these moments, she was not the little woman, but rather the aggressive provocateur. She experienced her husband's passivity as lack of interest and would often welcome exchanging beds with her child as a palliative to her pain of rejection. She began to question her own desirability as a woman and envied the warm reception accorded her daughter.

Aside from softening her displeasure and harsh, critical attitude toward herself and others, I also supported Mrs. S. in her capacity as parent to a curious young adolescent. For example, Susanna queried her mother about intimate bodily sensations as she identified the arousal of feelings in her clitoris (prickly) and vagina (velvety). Mrs. S. was able to share in these experiences and not withdraw from intimacy with her daughter. Recalling more pleasant past memories associated with her courtship, pleasurable bridal fantasies were aroused in both mother and daughter. Mrs. S's capacity to relax and welcome this exploration by her daughter further diminished Susanna's sense of alienation. At long last, she was beginning to let go of her fears and enjoy her developing body.

There were several instances recalled by mother and daughter that evoked guilt for Mrs. S. as well as anger. One of these provocative issues involved her lack of attunement to Susanna's emotional needs and poor decisions regarding childcare. These were difficult realities to confront, given Mrs. S's view of herself as reliable and responsible. Mrs. S. had selected Susanna's girlfriend's mother as an appropriate caregiver for her daughter while she was at work. It was this relationship with her girlfriend that fostered erotic play, including mutual masturbation and vaginal oral stimulation between the ages of 5 and 8 years. This highly charged play had been guarded as a secret by Susanna, disclosed only after departure of her father from the home. Reportedly, her girlfriend was the opposite of Susanna, described as athletic, aggressive, and an achiever at school. It appeared at first that Susanna had been "seduced and molested" by her friend, as she had been left by her mother, vulnerable to the wiles of others. However, as Susanna gradually revealed to her mother, the erotic play, sustained over a long period of time, may have been initiated by her friend with access to pornographic material; however, she, Susanna, also experienced the contact as pleasurable and became an active participant.

Prompted by these confrontations with her daughter, Mrs. S. was able to acknowledge she had left Susanna in compromising situations, unprotected from feelings of loneliness and the excitement of her sensitive body. Mrs. S's capacity not to retaliate with the shame or rage, that she certainly felt, or to become overwhelmed by guilt and self-recrimination were milestones in our work. She was able to understand Susanna's experiences as displaced longings for her and normal oedipal longings for her father. She understood that she had, on many occasions, not adequately protected Susanna by failure to set limits for her estranged husband and a paternal uncle who each played inappropriately with Susanna. Father and uncle each often violated her daughter's safe boundaries with provocative, intrusive, and aggressive play. Mrs. S. became aware of the difficulties for Susanna when she, Mrs. S., would allow her access to sleep in bed with her father on waking with fears at night. She began to explore her possible motivations for taking these actions and colluding in an active way to allow lacunae in protective boundaries. Mrs. S. came to better grasp the meaning of ambivalence and how these denied feelings can continue to influence actions. As she became able to understand the polarities in relationships that often coexist, she became more compassionate and understanding of her own and of her daughter's struggle. Susanna reciprocated by becoming a better partner at home, sharing responsibilities and daily routine chores.

As Mrs. S. came to accept her daughter for who she was and who she might become, there emerged between mother and daughter a new capacity for mutuality and compassion. Although complaints and anger needed tending, the work of mending in this mother–daughter relationship was clearly under way. Mrs. S. began to seek out new relationships with men and found one particular man she came to cherish. This man was very different from her first husband. He had many warm attributes; the couple had many interests in common and began a relationship that would end in marriage.

There is certainly much more that could be discussed about Susanna and her mother, both theoretically and technically, during this phase of simultaneous treatment. However, on the basis of these brief excerpts alone, it is clear that the experience of being in therapy with the same person enabled this dyad to progress from secrecy to confidentiality—from alienation to mutuality—and to sustain themselves during a time of crisis. They were each able to share with me separately, feeling secure I would safeguard their rights as individuals within the reality of their parent–child relationship. Processes of dissociation and denial had broken precious connections between mother and daughter. These missing links endangered Susanna's development and her acceptance of herself as a growing young woman. How in the future she would resolve defining her identity while coping with loss and her intense need for intimacy were to be lifelong challenges. However, in the short-term, simultaneous treatment, a supportive–expressive psychoanalytically oriented psychotherapy, helped both mother and daughter to use memory constructively to create a bond between them capable of enduring ambivalence and sustaining differences.

REFERENCES

Altman, N. (2000), Relational horizons in child psychoanalysis, *Journal of Infant, Child and Adolescent Psychotherapy,* 2(1):29–38.

_____, Briggs, R., Frankel, J., Gensler, D. & Pantone, P. (2002), *Relational Child Psychotherapy.* New York & London: Other Press.

American Psychiatric Association (2000), *Diagnostic and Statistical Manual of Mental Disorders* (4th ed, text revised). Washington DC: Author.

Bartram, P. (2003), Some oedipal problems in work with adopted children and their parents, *Journal of Child Psychotherapy,* 29(1):21–36

Benjamin, J. (1995), *Like Subjects, Love Objects.* New Haven, CT: Yale University Press

Blos, P. (1962), *On Adolescence.* New York: Free Press.

_____ (1980), Modifications in the traditional psychoanalytic theory of female adolescent development, *Adolescent Psychiatry,* 8:8–24.

Buirski, P. & Buirski, C. (1980), The split-transference in the simultaneous treatment of mother and child, *Bulletin of the Menninger Clinic,* 44:639–646.

Burlingham, D. (1951), Present trends in handling the mother–child relationship during the therapeutic process, *The Psychoanalytic Study of the Child,* 6:31–37. New Haven, CT: Yale University Press.

_____, Goldberger, A. & Lussier, A. (1955), Simultaneous analysis of mother and child, *The Psychoanalytic Study of the Child,* 10:165–186. New Haven, CT: Yale University Press.

Chazan, S. E. (2003), *Simultaneous Treatment of Parent and Child* (2nd ed.). London: Jessica Kingsley.

Chethik, M. (1976), Work with parents: Treatment of the parent–child relationship, *Journal of the American Academy of Child Psychiatry,* 15:453–563.

Edwards, J. & Maltby, J. (1998), Holding the child in mind: Work with parents and families in a consultation service, *Journal of Child Psychotherapy,* 24(1):109–33

Fast, I. (1984), *Gender Identity: A Differentiation Model.* Hillsdale, NJ: Analytic Press.

Freud, A. (1950), Introduction to simultaneous analysis of a mother and her adolescent daughter by Kata Levy, *The Psychoanalytic Study of the Child,* 15:378–380. New Haven, CT: Yale University Press.

Galenson, E. (1991), Treatment of psychological disorders in early childhood: A tripartite therapeutic model. In: *Beyond the Symbiotic Orbit,* eds. S. Akhtar & H. Parens, Hillsdale, NJ: Analytic Press.

_____ & Fields, B. (1989), Death of a young child's father: Effects on separation–individuation. In: *The Psychoanalytic Core: Essays in Honor of Leo Rangell, M.D.* Madison, CT: International Universities Press.

Green, V. (2000), Therapeutic space for re-creating the child in the mind of the parents. In: *Work with Parents: Psychoanalytic Psychotherapy with Children and Adolescents,* ed. J. Tsiantis. London: Karnac Books, pp. 25–45.

Hellman, I. (1960), Simultaneous analysis of mother and child, *The Psychoanalytic Study of the Child,* 15:359–377. New Haven, CT: Yale University Press.

_____ (1990), *From War Babies to Grandmothers.* London: Karnac.

Klauber, T. (1991), Ill treatment in the counter–transference: Some thoughts on concurrent work with an adopted girl and her family by the same psychotherapist, *Journal of Child Psychotherapy,* 17, 2, 45–60.

Kohn, B. (1976) Simultaneous analysis of child and parent by the same therapist, *Journal of the American Academy of Psychoanalysis,* 4:481–499.

Kolansky, H. & Moore, W. T. (1966). Some comments on the simultaneous analysis of a father and his adolescent son, *The Psychoanalytic Study of the Child,* 21:237–268. New Haven, CT: Yale University Press.

Lane, R. C. & Chazan, S. E. (1988), Psychoanalytic perspectives on the treatment of early adolescent girls, *Journal of Contemporary Psychotherapy,* 18:5–15.

Lassonde, S. & Mayes, L. (2005), Looking in and seeing out: Contexts of a longitudinal study in the age of Eisenhower. Unpublished manuscript. New Haven, CT: Yale University.

Levy, K. (1960), Simultaneous analysis of a mother and her adolescent daughter: The mother's contributions to the loosening of the infantile objective, *The Psychoanalytic Study of the Child,* 15:378–391. New Haven, CT: Yale University Press.

Novick, J. & Novick, K. K. (2001), Parent work in analysis. Part I: The evaluation phase, *Journal of Infant, Child and Adolescent Psychotherapy,* 1:55–57.

_____ (2002a), Parent work in analysis. Part II: Recommendation, beginning and middle phases of treatment, *Journal of Infant, Child and Adolescent Psychotherapy,* 2:1–27.

_____ (2002b), Parent work in analysis. Part III: Middle and pretermination phases of treatment, *Journal of Infant, Child and Adolescent Psychotherapy,* 2:17–42.

_____ (2002c), Parent work in analysis. Part IV: Termination and post-termination phases, *Journal of Infant, Child and Adolescent Psychotherapy,* 2:43–55.

Rustin, M. (1999), The place of consultation with parents and therapy with parents in child psychotherapy practice. In: *Handbook of Child and Adolescent Psychotherapy: Psychoanalytic Approaches,* eds. M. Lanyado & A. Horne. London: Routledge, pp. 87–92.

Shapiro, V., Fraiberg, S. & Adelson, E. (1980), Billy: Infant–parent psychotherapy on behalf of a child in a critical nutritional state. In: *Clinical Studies in Infant Mental Health,* ed. S. Fraiberg. New York: Basic Books, pp. 197–220.

Sholevar, G., Burland, J. A., Frank, J. L., Etezady, M. H. & Goldstein, J. (1989), Psychoanalytic treatment of children and adolescents, *Journal American Academy of Child and Adolescent Psychiatry,* 28;685–690

Slade, A. (1999), Representation, symbolization and affect regulation in the concomitant treatment of a mother and child, *Psychoanal. Inq.,* 19:797–830.

Sperling, M. (1950), Children's interpretation and reaction to the unconscious of their mother, *Internat. J. Psycho-Anal.,* 31:1–6.

_____ (1954), Reactive schizophrenia in children, *American Journal of Orthopsychiatry,* 24:506–512.

_____ (1970), The clinical effects of parental neurosis on the child. In E. J. Anthony and T. Benedek (eds.) *Parenthood.* Boston: Little Brown, pp. 539–570.

_____ (1982), A study of deviate sexual behavior in children by the method of simultaneous analysis of mother and child. In: *The Major Neuroses and Behavior Disorders in Childhood.* New York: Jason Aronson, pp. 243–270.

2 Fifth Ave.
New York, N.Y.10011
saraleachazan@aol.com

Bound Together by Chronic Pain and Trauma: A Study of Two Mother–Daughter Relationships

BARBARA S. SHAPIRO, M.D.

Girls and women are disproportionately affected by chronic pain unrelated to medically defined disease. Because the mother–daughter relationship is pivotal in female development, one can speculate that chronic pain could be entangled with and expressive of the mother–daughter relationship. I describe two women who came for treatment with chronic pain and other psychosomatic manifestations as the primary symptoms. Both experienced profound trauma and had deeply conflicted relationships with their mothers, in which reflective function and symbolic capacity were stunted, resulting in a physical language.

MOTHERS AND DAUGHTERS ARE CONNECTED IN MANY WAYS. THEIR bodies are similar, and they have physical experiences in common. The mother–daughter pair shares early intense attachments and multiple projections, identifications, and internalizations. These attachments and identifications are bidirectional and transgenerational. In the dyad, both partners shape the relationship (see Beebe and Lachman, 1997; Tronick, 2003).

The balance between merger and differentiation in the mother–daughter relationship varies with the dyad, time, context, culture, and development. However, mothers and daughters, no matter how dissimilar and differenti-

---

Barbara S. Shapiro, M.D. is an Associate Clinical Professor of Pediatrics and Psychiatry; University of Pennsylvania School of Medicine and Training and Supervising Analyst; Psychoanalytic Center of Philadelphia.

ated, recognize that they are also physically like one another. Sometimes boundaries become so porous that they may feel they are one another. This sort of partial or complete merger could be called "symbiosis, " although the term symbiosis is conceptually imprecise, whether applied to the early infant–mother dyad or later in the lifespan. What we often call symbiosis (see Mahler, 1975) is a state perhaps better characterized by some combination of the terms "boundarylessness," "undifferentiation," and "merger" (Pine 2004). Problems arise, however, in verbally describing individual variants of these nonverbal states. Merger, boundarylessness, and undifferentiation are related concepts, but can connote subtlety different aspects of these states. Therefore, for ease of communication, I use the term "symbiosis" in this article to describe the gestalt of these concepts.

States of merger and experiences of boundarylessness, first experienced in infancy, emerge in relationships and experiences throughout the lifespan. These states are an essential part of normal development and life experience. One hopes for a developmental evolution during the lifespan in which the potential for states of merger and boundarylessness is balanced with the potential for differentiation, individuation, and autonomy, to the extent helpful for that person, of that age and circumstance, in that culture. One also hopes for flexibility, so, for example, the girl–woman can, when necessary, experience a psychosomatic oneness with the other—for example, during pregnancy, childbirth, breastfeeding, and the sexual act.

The daughter is faced with the task of separating from a mother who is the first love object, a primary source of multiple psychic and somatic identifications and also a rival for the father (Bergman, 1987; Bergman and Fahey, 1996; Holtzman and Kulish, 2003). This is not always easy. Because of the thick and often conflicted constellations of attachments, likenesses, and identifications spanning the generations of women, the boundaries between mother and daughter, although certainly different in every dyad, can be porous, flexible, and ever changing when development is proceeding well (Chodorow, 1978).

As we well know, sometimes development does not proceed so well. The mother, while feeling an intense closeness with her daughter, must simultaneously hold in mind and nurture the psychic and somatic separateness of the daughter (see Coates, 1998). And the daughter, in addition to having the mother's blessing to separate, must have the constitutional and dynamic wherewithal to do so. Otherwise, the potential for symbiosis is perverted, and the relationship becomes a sticky mess, breeding irresolvable and unworkable conflicts of rage, hatred, rejection, humiliation, and malevolent envy.

Chronic illness in children and adolescents can powerfully affect many spheres of development. The physical dependence and care required in many illnesses complicates the balances of dependence and autonomy, merger and differentiation, intimacy and separation (Seiffge-Krenke, 1997). Because the mother is usually the primary physical caregiver for the ill child, the regression of illness focuses on that relationship. This situation can become further complicated when the child is a daughter, because of the simultaneous intense, mutually reinforcing pulls of attachment and identification and the porous boundaries between mother and daughter.

Deeply conflicted, ambivalent, and poorly differentiated relationships and their intrapsychic representations can feed illness. This process has been described in diabetes, asthma, inflammatory bowel disease, the painful "crises" of sickle cell disease, eczema, rheumatoid arthritis, chronic pain, and a variety of other illnesses and conditions (see Koblenzer, 1987; McDougall, 1989; Wilson and Mintz, 1989; Fonagy and Moran, 1994; Hogan, 1995; Shapiro et. al., 1995; Finell, 1997; Shapiro, 2003). This is not to say that the conflicts or self and object representations cause the illness. Rather, viewed within a biopsychosocial model, the expression of illness is influenced by a complex and unique convergence of biological, psychological, and social/cultural factors (Engel, 1980), with the relative influences of each varying within and among people.

In psychosomatic illness, physical and emotional factors are inextricably woven together. Symptoms become fixed and rigid, taking on a life of their own and taking over the life of the afflicted person. Chronic pain not associated with definable anatomic abnormalities or physical trauma is a common psychosomatic problem (Shapiro, 1995, 2003). In my experience working with people with chronic pain, both in private practice and in a pediatric pain program associated with a major tertiary care pediatric center, girls and women are disproportionately affected. Hypotheses about female vulnerability to chronic pain have included the tendency for girls and women to internalize; psychophysiologic differences in pain sensitivity, tolerance, and regulation; cultural forces; and the association of chronic pain with psychic trauma, including childhood abuse, with girls and women more likely to have been abused (Morris, 1991; Radomsky, 1995; Shorter, 1994). These hypotheses have, for the most part, been based on epidemiological data, short surveys or instruments, interviews, and sociologic observation. There are few reports of psychoanalytic material gathered from girls and women with chronic pain.

The mother–daughter relationship is pivotal in the lives of most women. Most—but not all—girls and women, in their psychoanalytic psychotherapies and analyses, spend considerable time and effort understanding and working through this relationship (Dahl, 1995). Thus it appears reasonable to speculate that debilitating chronic pain could be or become entangled with and expressive of the mother–daughter relationship.

I describe here two women in their relationships with their mothers. Each came to me with chronic pain and other psychosomatic manifestations as the primary symptoms prompting treatment. I present these cases to illustrate just some of the many ways the mother–daughter relationship and psychosomatic illness can be intertwined. For the purposes of discussion, I focus primarily on the mother–daughter relationship. Of course, that means that I have excluded the myriad of other equally significant issues that arose in treatment. In addition, both cases bring up many questions about the understanding and treatment of psychosomatic illness and trauma. The first case has the added complexity of memories of abuse that arose during the treatment and of multiple dissociated self-states. I have chosen not to discuss these and other potentially controversial aspects of the cases to maintain focus on the mother–daughter relationship.

The first patient was an adolescent when she started treatment, and so the real mother enters the discussion. The second patient was an adult. With her, I focus on the maternal aspects of the transferences.

Case #1

The First Session

I first saw Jenn when she was 15 years old. She was brought by her parents for her debilitating chronic pain.

In the very first evaluation session, Jenn's mother described her as having been "sick from the day she was born." She had been an irritable baby, seemingly "allergic to everything," and with a predilection for colds and other viral illnesses. The mother went on to describe how Jenn's multiple illnesses had interfered with school attendance starting in kindergarten. With the onset of puberty, Jenn developed diffuse muscle and joint pains, which slowly increased in severity. Over the year or two before I saw her, she spent most of her waking hours in bed, ate little, and was unable to leave the house for any activities. The mother described consultations with numerous physicians throughout Jenn's lifetime. They had reluctantly agreed to see me after a strong recommendation by a medical specialist they had consulted. No one in their family had ever seen a mental health professional.

I was immediately struck by Jenn's beauty—she had the face of a Botticelli angel. She was neatly dressed, her shirt ironed. Her body was thin, but not too thin, and she sat quietly, moving very little, and looking down at the floor. She made almost no eye contact, answered my questions in a soft, high-pitched, childlike voice, and had little to say except for describing her symptoms—and only when I asked her directly. She showed no emotion except for the tears that ran down her face when she described how terrible her pain was and how it was equally bad all over her body.

As is my usual custom for most adolescents with severe psychosomatic illness, for the initial evaluation I met with Jenn and her parents together. Jenn's mother, who answered most of the questions, was adamant that there were no emotional problems and that all Jenn's restrictions, including her inability to attend school, were because of severe pain and general predilection to illness. The father was withdrawn and noncommittal. When pressed, he stated that he thought his daughter was sick, but if she had more will power she could do more despite her illness. All members of the family were united in their anger at other health care professionals who either had not believed the severity of the pain, or who had offered no possible solutions.

The Initial Treatment

I accepted the family's perception that pain was the major problem and pointed out that it was profoundly affecting Jenn's life and development. We began treatment, agreeing that we would explore the pain, other physical symptoms, and related factors in the life of Jenn and her family. Jenn and her mother shared a profound mind–body split (Winnicott, 1964; Shapiro, 2003). Together they focused on the body. Because emotions and inner life were disavowed and inaccessible to me and to them, I had to enter their world speaking their language of the body. We agreed that Jenn would meet individually with me, once weekly, and that a colleague would meet with the family.

During the first months of treatment, Jenn spoke in a predictably sweet and concrete manner. She showed little insight into her symptoms or life situation. We talked about her pain, how she could not attend school, and how she was having trouble keeping up with her studies at home. I paid special attention to the severity of Jenn's symptoms and the degree of her distress. We tried adjunctive approaches, such as gentle physical therapy with a carefully chosen female physical therapist, and pharmacologic agents. These adjunctive measures helped only a small amount, but Jenn came to feel that I believed her pain and took her distress seriously and that I was not going to challenge her symptoms or experiences.

She described herself as having always been a sweet, obedient child, with neither anger nor anguish, and with no thoughts except those she perceived acceptable to her mother. Gradually, first tentatively and then in a tearful outpouring, Jenn described to me her despondency, the severe conflicts and daily fighting with her mother, her constant and overwhelming anxiety, and, ultimately, her pervasive and imminent suicidal thoughts and intent. It felt to me like a tidal wave of emotions erupting from a deceptively calm sea.

At this point, I discussed with Jenn whether and how she wanted her parents to understand the degree of her emotional anguish. We agreed that I would accompany her to a family therapy session. During the session, she described her anguish to her parents. Jenn's mother was initially shocked at the extent of her daughter's emotional distress. However, both parents eventually accepted that Jenn's problems affected her mind and not just her body.

Now our shared understanding of Jenn's symptoms was that they fell into two clusters—physical and emotional. The focus of treatment was on exploring and expanding the two spheres separately, rather than confronting or interpreting the mind–body split. Neither Jenn nor her mother perceived any relationships among her emotional distress, her severe and disabling pain, and her inability to attend school. Jenn's father agreed (although he remained quiet for the most part).

Jenn and I now had her mother's permission to explore the emotional sphere. Because of the extraordinarily close relationship between Jenn and her mother, this permission was essential to proceed. The process was very slow for several reasons. First, Jenn was at that time unable to express any disagreement with her mother or with me. I was concerned that she would agree with my interpretations, in a false-self compliance, resulting in a split off and inauthentic therapeutic process. Also, Jenn and her mother had sought medical advice from many different physicians over the prior years, and the family, as a whole, was quite mistrustful of mental health professionals. Having worked with many such patients, I knew that if I postulated links between mind and body before Jenn-and-her-mother were able to hear them, they were likely to flee treatment with me and seek more consultations and testing in the biomedical realm. Finally, approaching material expressed in the language of the mind without equally considering material expressed in the language of the body would have negated the most accessible realm of Jenn-and-her-mother's conscious experience.

I gradually introduced the possibility of mind–body interactions. Over time, Jenn began to make connections between physical and emotional symptoms. One day, about eight months after beginning treatment, in a remarkable leap forward, she told me that her inability to attend school was not because of pain, but rather because of longstanding severe anxieties, which she did not understand.

After Jenn made this crucial connection, I again accompanied her to a family therapy session. In the session she told her parents that it was her anxiety, and not her pain, that kept her from going to school. The mother at first protested, but then gradually accepted the connection. The mother's acceptance again gave Jenn and me permission to further explore connections between her somatic symptoms and her emotions and thoughts, both in the past and the present.

Jenn, her parents, and I were slowly establishing some trust and the beginnings of a therapeutic alliance. They no longer sought consultations from multiple medical specialists. After we discussed the need for Jenn to explore and understand her anxieties, they all agreed to my recommendation to increase the sessions to twice weekly.

Jenn's psychological symptoms rapidly increased in severity over the next several months. She had severe insomnia and repetitive nightmares of rape. Dissociative states occurred during the day, during which she would experience, as if real, the presence of a man who was raping her. She had episodes of uncontrollable rage, with destruction of physical objects in her environment. Jenn also described the emergence of voices, one male and the other female. The male voice urged her toward suicide, telling her that she was worthless. The female voice criticized everything she did. Jenn understood that the voices came from her, but that did not assuage the torment. I viewed the voices as representing savage and primitive superego introjects, and told Jenn and her parents, in responses to their questions, that she was in anguish for reasons we did not understand but was not psychotic.

Jenn's distress continued to escalate. About 1 year after treatment began, she experienced multiple pseudoseizures and episodes of bulimia. Her suicidal ideation was overpowering, and she made two suicidal gestures, followed by brief hospitalization. It became clear to Jenn, her parents, and me that hospitalization did not address her substantive chronic problems. All of us decided together that we would continue the psychotherapy and that the emotional and suicidal crises would be weathered at home, with the family providing safety (which, despite their problems, they were well able to do).

In the psychotherapy, exploration, insight, and understanding were accompanied by working on affect tolerance; awareness of mind, emotion, motivation, and agency; and self/other boundaries. Obviously, the holding environment and supportive approaches were necessary for this intensely distressed and suicidal adolescent. I avoided working in the transference, because Jenn's ability to play with reality and experience "as if" situations was shaky. It was difficult for Jenn and for me to contain the onslaught of material and crises in two sessions weekly. I recommended increasing the frequency, but Jenn's parents declined.

After months of anguish and distress, about fifteen months after we began treatment, one night Jenn told her mother of repeated severe physical, sexual, and emotional abuse by an older male relative, starting when she was about 4 or 5 years old, and continuing through early adolescence. Jenn's mother was aware of the controversy surrounding the emergence of memories of abuse. She called me to let me know what Jenn has said, that she and her husband believed Jenn, and that the details that Jenn shared were consistent with her memories and those of her husband. The older male relative was known to have abused drugs for years and to be deeply troubled and potentially violent. She wanted me to know this before I saw Jenn the following day.

With the emergence of this material, the parents agreed to increase the sessions to three times weekly. (However, because of external factors, my colleague was no longer available for family therapy.) Jenn described sexual abuse with oral sex and fondling starting around age 4. This progressed to a sadomasochistic relationship. For example, she described being beaten and burned with matches, and she detailed the relative's drunkenness and use of drugs. Jenn said the relative told her that if she told, no one would believe her and everyone would think she was a "dirty little girl." Jenn described suicidal thoughts starting at the age of 7. She wanted to be with the angels. She told how a presence called Bubba joined her when she was alone, soothing and comforting her. Jenn and her mother remembered that she did not grow normally between the ages of about 5 and 8, and this failure to thrive was the focus of medical concern. Jenn wondered why her parents never suspected that something other than physical illness was wrong. (Note: for reasons of confidentiality, I have left out salient aspects of what Jenn told me about the abuse. However, based on the extensive details supplied by Jenn and her parents over time, and on various clinical aspects of the situation, I believed that Jenn had been severely and chronically abused, that the male relative was the source of the abuse, and that the material was not immediately available because of a combination of repression, dissociation, and disavowal.)

The Question of Analysis

I had discussed analysis several times with Jenn and her mother. Jenn was interested but then decided against this step after discussion with her mother. The treatment introduced intense loyalty conflicts for Jenn and clearly threatened the exclusive and intense closeness between mother and daughter.

I knew by then that Jenn's mother did her homework for her, slept with her, told her what and when to eat, and generally structured her existence. Jenn hated this. However, at the same time, she and her mother saw any separation as abandonment and sense of separateness as self-annihilation. The two clung to each other. If Jenn's mother withdrew support in any way, Jenn's suicidality increased. I was often perplexed and overwhelmed by the intense suffering and ongoing torment. The necessity for suicide precautions made the condensed symbiosis and rapprochement conflicts extremely difficult to unravel and interpret.

Jenn reported that her mother usually told her what she should discuss in her sessions and asked for a reporting at home. Jenn's role in this gradually became apparent; she readily reported her session to her mother and asked her what she should discuss. Major issues often came up at home with her mother and not in the sessions with me. This included the emergence of various altered self-states. For example, Jenn talked frequently about "Cindy," describing the way she acted and what she said at home. We discussed some reasons why "Cindy" emerged at home and not with me, including feeling greater safety at home now that she had disclosed the abuse; her fear of separating from her mother and of feeling close to me; and the use of flashbacks, details of the abuse, and suicidality at home to gain her mother's attention and to punish her and me. Her mother, in turn, was still somewhat suspicious of the therapy and welcomed Jenn's confidences. I frequently wondered whose therapy it was and who was the therapist.

Jenn often asked her mother to join us for part or all of a session, particularly when the two of them were experiencing difficulties, when painful material was emerging, when Jenn was feeling rageful toward me, or when Jenn's safety or health were threatened in some way (e.g., with intense suicidal thoughts or plans). Over time, I appreciated more and more the extent of the boundarylessness between Jenn-and-her-mother. I began to wonder if I should change the frame and treat the actual symbiotic dyad, with the mother present in all or most of the sessions, rather than focusing on the individual work along with parental guidance and support. After struggling with this idea for some time, I saw potential benefits and losses on both sides, and eventually decided to talk about it with Jenn. She vigorously vetoed this possibility, saying that she needed time with me by herself if she was to have any hope of ever separating from her mother. After some discussion, we decided together to continue the same frame, with the focus on individual work, supplemented by joint sessions, most with Jenn and her mother, and some with both parents and Jenn. (Jenn had always been clear that she did not want me to meet with either of her parents without her.)

Jenn's mother was often understandably perplexed about how to handle difficult situations at home, such as Jenn's altered self-states, rages, suicidal gestures, and other problems. We often discussed, with Jenn present, how to think about and approach these problems. During sessions with Jenn and her mother, it became clear that Jenn's malevolent and punitive superego made her perceive her mother as a witch (Dahl, 1989). I believe the mother was aware of this, and her suspicion of me was in part her fear that I too regarded her as a witch. The joint sessions appeared to help the mother realize that I appreciated her difficulties in caring for Jenn and that I could see she loved and cared for her daughter. Both Jenn and I needed her mother's ongoing permission and support for treatment to continue.

One day Jenn demanded that her mother come into her session. After all three of us were seated, Jenn said that she was in an intolerable position between her mother and me and that she wanted the two of us to work it out. She then proceeded to say that she did not want to hear negative things about me at home. Her mother agreed. Jenn also said her mother was talking about decreasing her sessions and that this was not acceptable. The mother again agreed. I saw Jenn's courageous confrontation of the loyalty conflicts as signaling a beginning separation and individuation. This led, over the next few months, to Jenn and her parents deciding to start a four times weekly analysis.

The Analysis

The conversion from psychotherapy to analysis occurred approximately 2 years after the initial evaluation. It was relatively quiet, as Jenn was already coming three times each week, and our basic frame and mode of interaction remained the same. Rarely was she quiet within a session, although her mood and state varied widely within and between sessions. However, there were important qualitative changes. The sessions, although still tumultuous, were somewhat decompressed in intensity. Material that both of us knew had previously been avoided began to emerge. Because of the increased continuity and strength of the holding environment, we were able to work directly within the transference–countertransference matrix. The intersubjective realm became the fulcrum of treatment.

During one session, Jenn became quiet, put her head down, then jumped, looked startled, and began to talk like a child, appearing very disoriented. I asked, "What's happening?" Jenn asked in a childlike voice where she was and who I was. I answered, and remarked that this sounded like what she had told me was happening at home. She replied, "Jenny the 18 year old must have told you," and that she was 7 and her name was Cindy. After a while she said it was time for her to go and for "Jenny the 18 year old" to come back. Then she put her head down, was quiet for a minute, and appeared disoriented when she looked up and at me again. She asked if "Cindy" had been there. I told her exactly what I had observed of her behavior, not commenting on the meaning nor ascribing any label.

As the months and years progressed, various self-states began to make regular appearances in the sessions. At first these states usually emerged at home, with the mother. As time went on, some states appeared first with me. With the emergence of each state, I focused on exploring experiences, thoughts, and feelings within that state, the dynamics of why that state emerged at that particular time, and what the states represented. We began to see how the emergence of disparate states enabled Jenn to experience and express feelings and conflicts that were otherwise unspeakable. If, for example, Jenn became angry with her mother, one of the "alters" (Jenn's word) would emerge and throw shoes. Jenn pointed out the secondary gain of the child "alters" at home, saying, "My mom coddles them. She doesn't pay much attention to me." In a joint session, the mother acknowledged that this was the case. I also was aware of the countertransferential pull for me of the child self states.

After a while, it became clear that at home, Jenn-and-her-mother viewed and treated the self-states as discrete persons. I stated my view that these personae were all aspects of her self. I saw similarities between the way I worked with Jenn's self experiences and the way in which I work initially with people with chronic psychosomatic symptoms (Shapiro, 1995, 2003). I followed Jenn's lead in the choice of words and descriptors. For example, after she used the phrases "coming out" and "alters" several times with regard to the emergence of various self-states, I used those words in the same way. In general, in exploring, I used her words; in interpreting, I used words indicating the presence of a total self in addition to the split off parts. My aim was to enter into her experience and portrayal of the world while at the same time not reifying any particular aspect, similar to our previous work when her world consisted only of physical symptoms. (Note: Jenn's diffuse pain and other physical symptoms faded as various self-states emerged and generally became concentrated in a few "alters.")

A central theme of the analysis was Jenn's relationship with her mother. She stated that she and her mother were " … like twins—we feel the same. It is our life, not my life. " I replied that this closeness was both a burden and safety. She discussed her wish not to take such responsibility for her mother's well-being and to be her own self. She then got a small tattoo, which she saw as important for its symbolism in going against her mother's wishes, especially where her body was concerned. Later she told her mother, "As much as I love you I also hate you … I will have to deal with my anger toward you for me to go my own way."

Jenn gradually revealed the extent of physical closeness with her mother. They usually slept together, with their joint attention focused on the care and well-being of Jenn's body. Jenn longed for her mother's physical closeness. In addition, she had sexual fantasies about her mother and perceived her father as a rival. Sleeping together served to get her mother out of her father's bed. She also had fantasies about her father; keeping her mother out of the marital bed served to preserve her father for herself. Thus the problems in separation were both dyadic and triadic (Holtzman and Kulish, 2000).

Depression ricocheted around the family. When Jenn became profoundly depressed, her mother rallied and cared for her, her own depression appearing to improve. Other times, the mother was severely depressed herself. Each appeared to gain strength when the other was depressed. I pointed this out, first with Jenn, and then at her request in a joint session with her mother. I urged the mother to obtain psychotherapeutic help. She was resistant to the idea and resented the suggestion, saying that I was presumptuous and intrusive. Jenn said, "My mother says she will get better when I do." We agreed that this was quite a burden. Although the mother did not get treatment, we were able to ease some situations with the joint sessions.

My vacations and breaks were difficult for all of us. Jenn literally could not retain the image of a person who was gone. "First the sound of your voice goes. Then I cannot see you any more in my mind's eye. Then I get agitated and angry. Then you are just a name." Jenn and I called it "losing me in your mind's eye." One can speculate problems in object permanence as well as object constancy. Jenn reacted to upcoming separations not just with rage and terror but also with a dramatic increase in suicidality and regression of ego strength. Eventually we figured out that in Jenn's mind her suicidality simultaneously punished me for going away and ensured that I would be worried enough to keep her in my mind. This worked quite well; my concern and guilt kept her in the front of my mind. We related this enactment between Jenn and me to how Jenn used suicidality at home to punish and control her mother while also keeping her close. Jenn was convinced that the only way her mother continued to keep her in mind was to worry about her. Therefore she did whatever she felt was necessary in order not to lose her image of her mother having her in mind (see Coates, 1998; Fonagy and Target, 1998).

Jenn discussed how she would like to have her own life, separate from her mother but at the same time viewed any separation as abandonment and lack of caring by her mother. I remarked that the same thing happened in the analysis: she either felt controlled or abandoned by me and hated herself and me for both feelings. One day she reported a conversation that one of the altered self-states (Tina) had with her mother. Tina said that the mother had it "all wrong in regarding Jenn as weak and unable to do for herself." Tina pointed out that the mother left during the day for work, leaving Jenn to take care of herself, but then would sleep with Jenn at night when Jenn claimed that she was unable to sleep by herself. She told her mother that she should understand the difficulty but should not treat Jenn as if she were unable to do anything for herself. "Tell her she is strong enough to make it through the whole night alone. I've been waiting my whole life to hear this. It's always that I'm weak and crazy. You say you can't leave her. How can I feel strong?" (Note here the changes in who is designated as "I"—an indication of the dynamic shifts and permeability in the system of self-states.) After this discussion, Jenn began sleeping by herself most of the time, with a few regressions.

I was aware that Jenn and her mother were reading and discussing books on multiple personality disorder (MPD). Jenn was terrified that she had MPD. I empathized with her fears, discussed dissociative identity disorder and then asked whether there was another side to this—something positive for her. She talked about her need to have a name for what was wrong and to have a diagnosis. She associated to always being identified as the sick child, always taking and being given pills, always going to the doctor, and always having one diagnosis or another. "I always wanted to be sick rather than well. If you are well, they expect more of you." This feeling highlighted an important area, which we continued to explore: the wish for a diagnosis, the need to be labeled as very ill or crazy, the dangers involved in any improvement or strength. I speculated to myself that this provided a vehicle throughout Jenn's life for Jenn-and-her-mother, as a merged unit, to displace and project inner, undefined badness into a less-threatening, external, medicalized entity. The hatred of mind and intrapsychic contents was safely held by physician authorities within diagnoses. The projection and the search for a name also unified disparate and chaotic inner states.

Over time, we built a detailed picture of Jenn's development. Her mother had recurrent problems with depression, although they were never identified as such. The mother told Jenn and her siblings that all her problems started when the children were born. Jenn recalled her mother constantly crying in the kitchen when Jenn was very young. Jenn would pat her face and attempt to comfort her. "I would do anything to bring a smile to my mother's face." The mother reported that she never bonded with Jenn's older brother and sister but then felt intensely close to Jenn. She speculated that this was because of the effect of Jenn's numerous minor illnesses and allergies, which developed soon after birth.

Over the course of the analysis, it became clear that Jenn had never been able to separate from her mother. She and her mother recalled intense terrified screaming, to the point of exhaustion, at any brief separation or being put in her room to sleep at night. At the same time, as a toddler and young child, Jenn frequently wandered away from her mother, several times disappearing while on the beach or in a shopping center. She wished for her mother to come and find her but thought she would not notice her absence.

Other times she fantasized being found and adopted by a different and more loving family. In the sessions, running away emerged with certain "alters," who wished only to run away from where they were. Jenn noted that the feeling was the same as when she ran away as a small child. The running away and getting lost appeared developmentally related to the problems of the dyad in attachment, separation, and aggression (see Fonagy, 2001). Jenn became lost and was unable to find herself in her mother's mind's eye. At the same time, in her rage, she killed her internal image of her mother and lost the image of her mother in her mind's eye.

Jenn and her mother both experienced a great deal of difficulty regulating aggression—individually and as a dyad. Jenn reported her mother's frequent rages and related being hit and slapped and seeing the same happen with her siblings. Jenn herself had numerous prolonged and unmanageable temper tantrums, which disappeared totally after age 5 (perhaps when the abuse started). These tantrums and rage reactions later reemerged at home and in the sessions in the form of rageful and out of control "alters," seeking to torment, control, and abuse me. We talked about her fear of being like her mother in being unable to control her rage. She perceived that her rage was responsible for her mother's depression and unavailability. She also felt that if her mother had not been depressed she would have prevented the abuse.

After several years of analysis, Jenn questioned why her mother turned to her for solace and not to her husband. She talked about this with her father and told him that the mother's welfare was his responsibility, not hers. The symbiosis between mother and child both created and was enabled by the father's lack of involvement.

Case #2

Four days each week, I heard Pat's sneakered feet slowly plodding across the carpet to my door. She would knock softly, peer around the corner, and glance at me as she shuffled into the room. Sometimes she smiled slightly—more often as the analysis progressed. She would lower herself painfully into a chair. (She could not lie on the couch.) After a short pause, she would speak—her voice low, quiet, even. If the heat was blowing, I had to lean forward to hear her. For two years, she started with a comment about a physical symptom. Then her first words started to change—sometimes her daughter, sometimes a symptom, sometimes a complaint about her parents or her husband. As the session would proceed, her words gathered force, with little change in her tone. Usually she would end up, in one way or another, talking about her mother. She told heart-rending tales of abandonment, abuse, bitterness, hopelessness, isolation, and despair—and sometimes of hope, love, pride, and beauty. Her words and phrases were articulate, poetic, evocative, and aloof. Occasionally she cried silently. As soon as I would announce the end of the session she would stop, get up with her head bowed, and plod back to the door. Our eyes would meet in a fleeting glance. "So—see you tomorrow?" she would murmur deferentially. "Yes, tomorrow," I would reply. We then would nod, our gazes would meet again, and she would leave.

The Beginning

Pat was 39 when her physical therapist, concerned and frustrated by Pat's unremitting chronic pain, referred her to me. She came with some trepidation, as she had sought psychotherapeutic help from men before but never from a woman. Pat got along better with men. She was concerned that her relationship with her mother would pollute her ability to work with a woman. However, at the same time she was desperate and knew I had experience working with people with chronic pain.

When I first saw Pat, she moved slowly, stiffly, with obvious pain. Her face was masklike and downcast. I winced on seeing her. She was house bound, able to walk only a block, very slowly. Her days were consumed by stretching and icing her painful muscles. She was considering using a wheelchair.

Background

The pain started when Pat was in her late twenties. She and her husband had moved across the country from her parents. Pat, a bright, articulate woman who did well in school, decided to go to law school. One day she shared her plans with her mother, who was visiting. Her mother said, "You can't do that. That means you won't be able to take care of me." The pain started a few days after this conversation, and in a few months had spread all over her body. It continued to worsen.

Pat's father was alcoholic and physically abusive to her mother. Her mother was deeply sadistic, self-involved, and depressed, and she had attempted suicide on numerous occasions. The mother had another daughter by a prior marriage, whom she had given away at the age of 3 years and never saw again. The mother herself had chronic severe pain. The problems spanned the generations. Pat's maternal grandmother had died when her mother was 3 years old. The grandfather remarried; Pat's mother described her stepmother as physically abusive and cold.

Pat remembered that when she was 3, her mother became withdrawn, sometimes not speaking. She beat Pat fiercely and often, prompting complaints from the neighbors. Then, when Pat was 6, her father left to serve in the military. Pat's mother abruptly and without explanation sent her to an orphanage, where she stayed for six months until her father returned from the war. No one in the family ever spoke of the orphanage or offered Pat any explanation.

After Pat returned from the orphanage, the house was filled with fighting, physical violence, and cold silences. Her father told her she was to blame for the mother's suicide attempts, and the mother told Pat that she was responsible for her (the mother's) happiness. Pat described being used as an object for her mother's rage, contempt, and envy. She recalled no humor or laughter in her house and reported that her mother, who could be very charismatic, laughed with others and then when back home became silent and rageful with her daughter.

According to Pat, her mother loved babies until they showed "a mind of their own." Her mother had boasted about feeding her cream as a baby so she would be as fat as possible. Pictures confirmed that Pat was indeed a fat baby. The mother herself was anorectic, and after babyhood often did not feed Pat adequately. "I would be starving between meals and would steal plums from the trees. Then at meals she would stuff me." Pat speculated that her mother could not abide Pat's becoming her own person as she grew out of babyhood. She linked this to the mother's abandonment of Pat's half sister when the sister was 3. Initial boundarylessness during infancy was followed by overt rejection and hatred at the first signs of differentiation and individuation.

The dyad was filled with envy. Pat's mother disparaged and attacked any areas in which Pat showed ability and interest, such as ballet, schoolwork, and art. Later, when Pat had a boyfriend, the mother asked to speak to him alone and persuaded him to break up with Pat. Pat had trouble seeing her own envy and contempt, but one day described walking next to her mother when she was 10, assessing her mother's slim but feminine body. They were dressed in identical spaghetti strap sundresses, which her mother had made. Pat felt a sense of superiority—that her slim, hard, flat-chested body looked better in the dress than her mother's.

The Analysis

I began Pat's treatment with some apprehension. I was relieved when she talked and talked, with evident relief. Her symptoms lessened and her function improved. We developed a solid therapeutic alliance. I often felt like a nonperson. I liked Pat and was drawn into her eloquent and evocative word images.

Pat feared that I would either attack her or leave her. "In the meantime," she said, "I will make hay while the sun shines." I saw the "making hay" as a metaphor for her islands of resilience and strength; she had been able to take advantage of small opportunities for positive interactions during her development.

Her transferences were reflected in the many dreams she had about our relationship:

> She dreamed she was on the beach and saw some shards from green glass bottles. The shards looked smooth and inviting but in reality were sharp and would cut if she picked them up. She associated to her fear of the analysis and me; she felt plunged into a darkness in which she could no longer see or anticipate dangerous objects.
>
> She dreamed that she went into a public bathroom and saw an apparently normal woman at the sink. The woman looked up and she had no face, only slits for eyes. Then the woman laughed, ripped off a mask, exposing a monstrous face.

A central conviction emerged—that I, like her mother, was unreliable and likely to be cruel and abuse her, and, therefore, the safest course was to rely only on herself. This protected her from betrayal, overwhelming disappointment, and abandonment. She literally had no expectations of me and so literally did not feel abandoned, disappointed, or angry. "I accept that you are irrelevant." We discussed the threat of destruction with any hint of anger or frustration—destruction of her, me, or both of us. She stressed the futility of allowing herself to experience painful feelings, which would have no impact on my actions, like my going away for holidays.

She said one day "I live between fury and terror." Indeed that appeared to be the case, with the key word being "between," as the zone between was devoid of words, intense feelings, and the fury and terror that lived between us were seen and experienced by her and me as omnipresent but in the distance. She put up walls of thick soft cotton to keep me at a safe distance, absorbing the intensity of sound and movement and yet also cushioning against what was clearly a greater danger—that we would be close enough to destroy one another, like her and her mother.

Despite all this, she reported progress. She went to the movies for the first time in 10 years—and enjoyed it. She and her family vacationed at the beach, and, for the first time in years, she was able to walk on the sand up to the water without undue pain. Her home rituals of icing and stretching quietly receded, taking less time.

Over time, a new element was introduced into the sessions. This consisted of rhapsodic, detailed, and moving descriptions of small things that brought pleasure and beauty into her life—for example, her garden and her bonsai. She described transforming a small plot of dirt into a blooming and colorful rose garden. I responded with delight, and she and I spoke of transformations and change, staying within the metaphor. This was the counterpoint to the negative and traumatic transferences and enabled us to continue.

The Illnesses

Her illnesses kept us at a distance. Pat had a history of allergies, asthma, and bronchitis. However, starting in the second year of analysis, these symptoms and ailments started to cascade. She developed disabling episodes of chronic and recurrent sinusitis, accompanied by severe asthma. She had sinus surgery, with a difficult postoperative course. She developed a cyst in her hard palate, which had to be removed surgically, hemorrhagic uterine bleeding, and assorted other serious problems. At times, various muscle groups would go into painful immobilizing spasm, and she would stay locked for days and sometimes weeks. She missed many sessions, sometimes more than one or two weeks at a time, because of the illnesses and pain. She said one day while leaving my office "You had better fix your heat or you will kill all your patients and then you won't have anyone." I was the sadistic, murderous, intrusive, and neglectful mother against whom she had no recourse other than to maintain both physical and psychic distance.

I pondered whether the analytic material was deepening too rapidly, contributing to changes in her immune system and spasm of smooth muscles. A psychosomatic split serves primitive defensive functions, and we were bridging this split around the area of her pain. At the same time, I realized that these problems were tormenting and binding her and that this turn of events was expected and perhaps necessary in Pat's analysis. The psyche and the soma, divided, must enter the analytic room, unified within the transference–countertransference matrix, or else the mind–body split will be eternal.

Pat related her asthma and her anger. "I can't get angry when I can't breathe." I remarked on her perception of her anger as destructive to herself or to others. She said, "My insides are being eaten away by the bitterness. If I live long enough, perhaps something will happen to the people who have it so good." When I asked about her feeling while talking about this she replied, "A feeling in my chest—like I can't breathe."

She then spoke of the life and death struggle between her and her mother, in which she was responsible for keeping her mother from committing suicide and at the same time they hated one another. "It's as if my hands are around her neck and her hands are around my neck, choking me. Neither of us can let go because the other would win." This vivid image became part of our analytic repertoire.

Pat described her mother as occasionally warm and loving. During those interludes she would be "seduced" by the possibility of safety and love. Rage and abuse would quickly and unpredictably destroy the warmth, but during the good periods, Pat would suspend her anticipation of what was to come. "I become undone by the smallest kindnesses that come my way. It's like instant glue, and simultaneously fear and the wish to get away."

She feared losing her self-identity if she felt love—with her mother and with me. Somehow she fought back, and through anger maintained a sense of self. However, she said, humiliated by her longing, "If she had offered me love, I would have given my self up for it."

These dynamics were reflected in the transference. Her warm feelings for me evoked the wish for and fear of merger, along with humiliation, rage, and terror that she or I or both of us would be destroyed. She responded by establishing a safe psychic and somatic distance. Talking about this she said, "It's like a planet revolving around the sun. As you get close, the warmth is lovely, so you get even closer. Then it gets too hot, hurts, and you go away. But then it gets cold and dark and you turn around to get close again."

Pat came into one session complaining about a muscle spasm that started after the prior session. "If what I say here is going to make me limp, the idea is to get better, not to disable me." I commented on her perception that I was making bad matters worse. She said, "I'm the one who has to pay. It's like with my physical therapist. She got to go home to her nice home, and I would suffer. There is no safety net. Yet staying where I am is no solution." I was the toxic mother, living the good life while poisoning her body with my words and by my very existence. The transference–countertransference matrix became a life and death struggle, in which her body was "a monster—requiring all this time."

The Pain

Pat suffered and she endured her suffering. Nowhere was this more evident than in her perpetual pain. The pain, along with her relationship with her mother, was one of the organizing themes of the analysis.

We saw how the pain motif intertwined with many aspects of her relationship with her mother. In her pain, she was like her mother, who also had chronic pain. She felt herself to be intertwined with her mother and at times was not sure of the difference. Pat noted that her mother had expected to die at age 30 (she did not); this was frequently discussed within the family. Pat's life "blew apart" when she was 30. She spoke of her mother as her "… mirror … my mother and I will die at the same time … our symptoms are uncanny mirrors of one another … I got depressed for the first time after she was very depressed … I was locked in with her and had to die if she did. After all I was her little ray of sunshine, and if she were depressed it was my fault."

Pain served a fantasized masochistic function. "My mother said I was a bad child and now I have pain … she said I don't deserve a husband or my home or a child … what she can do I cannot do … I am not allowed … my mother wants my suffering as her present from me." Pain protected against the double-edged threat of failure and of surpassing her mother. Significantly, she developed pain after announcing to her mother her plans to go to law school (see Moulton, 1975). Pain kept her from having to visit her mother and care for her when her mother became ill.

Pat identified some of the pain as remembered sensations from the past (see Hopenwasser, 1998). For example, both her shoulders were frozen, and the degree of immobility was resistant to the best efforts of the physical therapist. When discussing this she said, "Maybe this is a crazy idea, but the feeling in my shoulders is just like the feeling I had when my mother would be hitting me and I would drop my arms and keep them immobile in order to avoid hitting her back." We discussed how the pain was both a body memory and a protection against loss of control over her rage.

Discussion

Some occurrences of psychosomatic illness have been described as "one mind in two bodies" (McDougall, 1989; Seiffge-Krenke, 1997). This expression richly evokes the symbiotic aspect of the mother–daughter relationship in these situations. However, it leaves out other aspects, such as tormented conflicts in the dyad and the triad, involving aggression, humiliation, rage, malevolent envy, rejection, and hatred. Psychosomatic illness is highly complex, overdetermined, and multifaceted, as is the mother–daughter relationship. Therefore, I present these cases not to generalize about that which is fluid and highly complex but to illustrate a few of the myriad ways that psychosomatic illness and the mother–daughter relationship can be entangled.

Jenn clearly was a vulnerable child before the abuse. She probably had some constitutional difficulties affecting psychophysiologic regulation, conflated with the problems in attachment and interactional patterns with a depressed and intermittently explosive mother (see Tronick and Weinberg, 1997; Fonagy, 2001). The father was both uninvolved and excluded. Thus he was not able to serve the potential role of the second parent in loosening the highly conflicted and yet gratifying symbiosis between the child and the primary early care-giving parent. By history, the attachment sounds disordered and chaotic. This, along with the severe trauma, is consistent with Jenn's lack of self and object constancy and profound dissociation of multiple selves (Cicchetti and Toth, 1995). The mother's depression continued throughout Jenn's life. Early patterns of interaction could not be reworked during later developmental phases, and without the interactional and protosymbolic basis for forming a coherent sense of self, Jenn could not navigate separation and individuation, regulate aggression, or achieve object constancy. The mother's own relational problems, family dynamics, and transgenerational patterns also maintained the symbiotic bond between mother and child (Fraiberg et al., 1975; Hesse and Main, 1999). Illness became the glue for the dyad and for Jenn's chaotic sense of self. The illness strengthened the father's exclusion, removing him as a rival for each member of the dyad.

Trauma further fragmented Jenn's experience of herself and others, interfered with libidinal development, introduced insolvable oedipal conflicts, and strengthened her sadomasochistic solutions. Dissociation of self and affective states was defensive, expressive, and functional developmentally. The dissociation between mind and body was a major defense of the mother–daughter dyad and served to maintain the merged state while projecting the hatred and aggression into the illness.

By contrast, Pat most likely was born with a constitutional resilience (Weil, 1970). She described herself as "one of those people who can soak up any little hint of warmth that comes along." Although there were few favorable developmental opportunities and objects, she took advantage of each of them. Yet, external impediments to her development were profound. Her mother never saw her as a separate and feeling being but rather as a repository for the mother's hatred of her own mother and stepmother and of herself. She was able to care for Pat's body during infancy, although she stuffed her with calorie-laden and nutrient-poor cream. The anorexic mother made her baby fat. Pat's strivings for independence and self-expression were anathema. She was overtly and clearly rejected, malevolently envied, and hated by her mother. In turn, Pat hated and envied her mother while longing for her approval.

The symbiosis between Jenn and her mother was ongoing, although conflicted by hostile aggression, rage, and guilt. For Pat, symbiosis dissolved and was replaced by a sadomasochistic struggle to the death, which kept mother and daughter close but not merged. The one was selfish love; the other was selfish rivalry (Bergman, 1987). The pain served different functions in each dyad.

Overall, these two cases illustrate two tormented and traumatized mother–daughter dyads. For both, the body was a primary arena of suffering and expression. Both mothers were depressed, affecting the daughters at all stages of development, including early attachment and interactional patterns. The daughters felt responsible for their mothers' depression and well-being. Their guilt was profound. Both dyads were locked into a rapprochement-like struggle, and both were caught in unworkable triadic passions and rivalries.

In both relationships, for developmental and conflictual reasons, self and other could not be regarded as integrated thinking, feeling persons. Reflective function and symbolic capacity were stunted, resulting in a physical language (Bucci, 1997). These developmental problems spanned the generations.

REFERENCES

Beebe, B., Lachman F. & Jaffe J. (1997), Mother–infant interaction structures and presymbolic self and object representations, *Psychoanal. Dial.,*7:133–182.

Bergman, A. (1987), On the development of female identity: Issues of mother–daughter interaction during the separation–individuation phase, *Psychoanal. Inq.,* 7:381–396.

_____ & Fahey, M. (1996), Two women and their mothers: On the internalization and development of mother–daughter relationships, *J. Amer. Psychoanal. Assn.,* 44S:449–482.

Bucci, W. (1997), Symptoms and symbols: A multiple theory code of somatization, *Psychoanal. Inq.,* 17:151–172.

Chodorow, N. (1978), *The Reproduction of Mothering: Psychoanalysis and the Sociology of Gender.* Berkeley; University of California Press.

Cicchetti, D. & Toth, S. (1995), Child maltreatment and attachment organization. In: *Attachment theory: Social, Developmental, and Clinical Perspectives,* ed. S. Goldberg, R. Muir, & J. Kerr. Hillsdale, NJ: The Analytic Press, pp. 279–308.

Coates S. (1998), Having a mind of one's own and holding the other in mind, *Psychoanal. Dial.,* 8:115–148.

Dahl, E. K. (1989), Daughters and mothers: Oedipal aspects of the witch mother, *The Psychoanalytic Study of the Child,* 44:267–280. New Haven, CT: Yale University Press.

_____ (1995), Daughters and mothers, *The Psychoanalytic Study of the Child,* 50:187–204. New Haven, CT: Yale University Press.

Engel G. (1980), The clinical application of the biopsychosocial model, *Amer. J. Psychiat.,* 137:535–544.

Finell J. (1997), *Mind–Body Problems: Psychotherapy with Psychosomatic Disorders.* Northvale, NJ: Jason Aronson, Inc.

Fraiberg S., Adelson E. & Shapiro V. (1975), Ghosts in the nursery: A psychoanalytic approach to the problems of impaired infant–mother relationships, *J. Amer. Acad. Child Psychiat.,* 14:387–421.

Fonagy P. (2001), *Attachment Theory and Psychoanalysis.* New York; Other Press.

_____ & Moran G. (1994), Psychoanalytic formulation and treatment: Chronic metabolic disturbance in insulin-dependent diabetes. In: *The Imaginative Body,* eds. A. Erskine, D. Judd. Northvale, NJ: Jason Aronson Inc., pp 60–86.

_____& Target M. (1998), Mentalization and the changing aims of child psychoanalysis, *Psychoanal. Dial.,* 8:87–114.

Hesse, E. & Main, M. (1999), Second-generation effects of unresolved trauma in nonmaltreating parents: Dissociated, frightened, and threatening parental behavior, *Psychoanal. Inq.,* 19:481–540.

Holtzman D. & Kulish N. (2000), The feminization of the female Oedipal complex, Part I: A reconsideration of the significance of separation issues, *J. Amer. Psychoanal. Assn,* 48:1413–1437.

_____ (2003), The feminization of the female oedipal complex Part II: Aggression reconsidered, *J. Amer. Psychoanal. Assn,* 51:1127–1151.

Hogan, C. (1995), *Psychosomatics, Psychoanalysis, and Inflammatory Disease of the Colon.* Madison, WI: International Universities Press.

Hopenwasser, K. (1998), Listening to the body: Somatic representations of dissociated memory. In: *Relational Perspectives on the Body,* eds. L. Aron & F. Anderson. Hillsdale NJ: The Analytic Press, pp. 215–236.

Koblenzer, C. (1987), *Psychocutaneous Disease.* Orlando, FL: Grune and Stratton, Inc.

Mahler, M. S., Pine, F. & Bergmann, A. (1975). *The Psychological Birth of the Human Infant: Symbiosis and Individuation.* New York: International Universities Press.

McDougall, J. (1989), *Theaters of the Body: A Psychoanalyst's Approach to Psychosomatic Illness.* New York: Norton and Co.

Morris, D. (1991), *The Culture of Pain.* Berkeley: University of California Press.

Moulton, R. (1975), The effect of the mother on the success of the daughter, *Contemp. Psychoanal., 21:266–282.*

Pine, F. (2004), Mahler's concepts of "symbiosis" and separation–individuation: Revisited, reevaluated, and redefined, *J. Amer. Psychoanal. Assn.,* 52:513–533.

Radomsky, N. (1995), Lost Voices: Women, Chronic Pain and Abuse. New York: Harrington Park Press.

Seiffge-Krenke, I. (1997), "One body for two" The problem of boundaries between chronically ill adolescents and their mothers, *The Psychoanalytic Study of the Child,* 52:340–355. New Haven, CT: Yale University Press.

Shapiro, B. (1995), Treatment of chronic pain in children and adolescents, *Pediatric Annals,* 24: 148–156.

_____ (2003), Building bridges between body and mind: The analysis of an adolescent with paralyzing chronic pain, *Int. J. Psychoanal.,* 84:1–15.

_____, Dinges, D., Orne, E., Bauer, N., Reilly, L., Whitehouse, W. Ohene-Frempong, K. & Orne, M. (1995), Home management of sickle cell related pain in children and adolescents: Natural history and impact on school attendance, *Pain,* 61:139–144.

Shorter, E. (1994), *From the Mind into the Body: The Cultural Origins of Psychosomatic Symptoms.* New York: The Free Press.

Tronick, E. (2003), "Of course all relationships are unique": How co-creative processes generate unique mother–infant and patient–therapist relationships and change other relationships, *Psychoanal. Inq.,* 23:473–491.

_____ & Weinberg, M. K. (1997), Depressed mothers and infants: Failure to form dyadic states of consciousness. In: *Postpartum Depression and Child Development,* eds. L. Murray & P. Cooper. New York: Guilford Press.

Weil, A. (1970), The basic core, *The Psychoanalytic Study of the Child,* 25:442–460. New Haven, CT: Yale University Press.

Wilson, P. & Mintz, I. (1989), *Psychosomatic Symptoms: Psychodynamic Treatment of the Underlying Personality Disorder.* Northvale, NJ: Jason Aronson.

Winnicott, D. W. (1964), Psycho-somatic disorder. In: *D. W. Winnicott Psychoanalytic Explorations,* ed. C. Winnicott, R. Shepherd, & M. Davis. Cambridge, MA: Harvard University Press (1989), pp. 103–118.

1826 Delancey Place
Philadelphia PA 19103
barbarashapiro@earthlink.net

The Disappearing (or Ghost) Mother Transference: In Search of the Available Mother Within

SHARON ZALUSKY, PH.D.

As analysts, we speak of maternal transference as if it were a unitary phenomenon. We are trained to expect intense, powerful transference reactions. Yet there is a group of female patients who have a specific type of transference that lacks intensity. These patients often present by not presenting. I term this phenomenon the *disappearing (or ghost) mother transference.* This transference is quiet and does not create much stress. Using a case example, I will define this particular type of object relationship and discuss an alternative technique in treating these patients. It is my premise that these women must discover for themselves, at their own time and in their own way, the caring, living, available mother in the analyst.

As analysts, if we do not know intuitively, we soon learn from our patients there are many ways to be a mother and to be mothered (Zalusky, 2000). Yet when we talk about maternal transference or maternal countertransference, we often speak about it as if it were a unitary phenomenon, even though we are fully aware an individual mother's mothering ability may change during different developmental stages, both her own and those of her children.

The type of mothering a woman gives is naturally affected by her own temperament, personality, history, life situations, stressors, unconscious conflicts, views about gender, birth order, therapy, and how all of these and

Sharon Zalusky, Ph.D., is faculty and member of the New Center for Psychoanalysis and is faculty and member of the California Psychoanalytic Society.

other factors interact with similar and different variables in her child. At times in the psychoanalytic literature,[1] and certainly in our practices, we find more specific types of maternal transferences. Occasionally, we speak of the hostile maternal transference, the phallic maternal transference, and the erotic maternal transference. All of these transferences express the patient's intense psychic engagement with the mother–analyst. In this article, I would like to report, however, on a different type of analytic engagement that I have seen repeatedly in various degrees in my clinical practice. Rather than intensity, the women patients I am reporting on present almost with a take-it-or-leave-it attitude toward the analysis. Yet, curiously, these patients are not indifferent. They are concerned about their own welfare. During the actual sessions, they are often involved in the analytic work. Many of the patients are, by anybody's account, kind, caring people. They do not appear to be either overtly or covertly hostile to the analysis. They simply do not appear to care whether they come to sessions or not. During weekends, holidays, business trips, or cancellations, they are perfectly content and do not appear to miss, let alone suffer longings for, their analyst or their analysis. Their general attitude toward me, their analyst, can be characterized as friendly, even warm, but I am only a small part of their often very busy life. Although the analysis may be important to these patients, what is most notable is that the analytic relationship is not intense. In this article, I intend to describe what, on the surface, appears to be a puzzling transference and to discuss a departure from ordinary procedure required to treat it.

As analysts, we are trained to expect intensity. We look for powerful transference reactions, and when we do not find these intense emotional responses, our theory tells us that our patients must be defending against them. If the feelings are not there, we have been taught to believe they must be unconscious (Renik, 1994, 1998), or our patients are using us as a selfobject function. If we, the analysts, have strong reactions to our patients seemingly not having responses to breaks in the analytic frame, our theory suggests that the intensity of our feeling is frequently not our own, but caused by our patient's projective identification. We are taught an analyst-centered view, which often presumes the patient's unconscious feelings about separation when they may not actually exist. I am asserting that such an approach in this type of transference may lead the analyst away from

[1]In the latest Psychoanalytic Electronic Publishing CD Rom the generic term *maternal transference* is cited 292 times.

truly understanding and helping these unusual patients. By not adjusting our technique, we risk embarking on a destructive impasse.

In this article on mothers and daughters, I would like to look at this phenomenon that I will refer to as the *disappearing (or ghost) mother transference.* It can be characterized by the lack of intensity in the transference. We would be making a mistake if we were to see this simply as a defense against the transference, for this lack of intensity may very well represent a specific type of object relationship and therefore be its own type of transference. Although I call this the disappearing (or ghost) mother transference paradoxically, in the treatment setting it is not the mother–analyst who vanishes, but the patient who intermittently goes away.

In the past few years, I have treated a number of women[2] with varying degrees of difficulty, who present by not presenting. They believe it does not make a difference if they come or not. They cannot imagine that it matters to me. Instead of hating me for their belief that it has no real meaning to me whether they come or go, they take it in stride. It is the world as they know it—a world they adapted to a long time ago. I believe it is necessary to differentiate these women from others whose adaptation is part of an "as if" or narcissistic personality disorder. For the most part, these women are psychologically sophisticated. They are quite capable, when not under emotional distress, of understanding the motivation of others. People are not used primarily as selfobjects in an attempt to regulate their sense of self. If anything, these patients are too separate from others, not fully able to appreciate the basic intersubjective nature of all relationships.

I group these women together, because they have several things in common. On the outside they are all intelligent, thoughtful, kind people who are capable of achievement, but inside they are often plagued by low self-esteem. They have friends and lovers, though their relationships may lack intimacy. These women are experts at subordinating their own desires and, because of this, have had difficulty in self-definition. They are often adaptive. Each of these patients has had by all standards a decent, kind mother who because of illness (either her own or that of a close relative), psychological problems, or stress was not able to be emotionally present even while most of the time being physically present. Each has had a father who has not been able to compensate for the mother's shortcomings be-

[2]I have also treated some men who present with a similar dynamic, but because this edition focuses on mothers and daughters, I will describe how this dynamic has played out with my female patients.

cause he, too, was absent due to of illness, work, war, or just difficulty relating to young children. These patients are notably sweet, because they have been treated sweetly, but often it has been by rote, by mothers who do not intimately know their children or even know to know their children. My patients grew, developed, and adapted in spite of this but at a cost to their own well-being. I underline the basic sweetness of these patients, because I believe that is how they differ from other patients of mine who have developed a more paranoid style of relating in response to their needs not being adequately attended to. The angry, hostile, paranoid patient is one that the analytic literature appears to favor. That may be because the angry patient is always involved with us. They keep us continually present albeit through their anger and disappointment. No matter how we fail them, they rarely miss sessions and almost always work in the transference (at least in the way we have defined transference). As analysts, we viscerally feel these patients' connection to us. It is as if we are comfortable with patients who conform to our theory and to our structure, even, or maybe especially, if they are loud and noisy about it.

The transference I am about to describe is different. It is quiet without much apparent stress in the relationship. In the following, I will describe my patient Suzie. She is not the first of my patients who has presented like this, but 2 years into the analysis, she presented us with a dilemma that obligated me to think about this phenomenon in a different way than I had been trained to do. Treatment, as I will discuss, consisted of her need to find and refind, the mother–analyst over and over again where she did not expect me to be—there, present, and under her control.

It is my premise that these women must discover for themselves at their own time and in their own way the caring, living, available mother in the analyst.[3] Because these patients do not always come consistently to treatment, I believe it requires a certain flexibility on the part of the analyst to keep the treatment going. Adjustment in technique is often required. These patients may need to come and go on their own schedule: feeding on demand as opposed to feeding on schedule. If not, they may submit to us in the hope of getting their needs met or they may leave the analysis. We analysts may mistakenly conclude that these patients were either not analyzable or did not want to be helped.

[3]Glen Gabbard mades a similar point in his plenary address, "On gratitude and gratification" at the spring meeting of the American Psychoanalytic Association in Washington. D.C., May 15, 1999.

In this volume on mothers and daughters, I believe this phenomenon has special meaning. Many of these women are either mothers or will become mothers during or after treatment. In helping our patients understand the meaning of the disappearing mother to their own internal development, we help them create both internally and externally an available mother who is able to attend to the needs of the inner child and, consequently, to the needs of their actual daughters and sons.

Case

Suzie is an attractive married woman now in her late thirties who began an analysis 8 years ago during a time of great stress. By anybody's standard but her own, Suzie is a highly intelligent, accomplished person. It is noteworthy that she is a pioneer who has achieved a singular place in history. Suzie's colleagues, friends, and acquaintances include some of the most noted, powerful, creative, and interesting people in the world. She moves between many worlds literally and figuratively. Her own personal experiences have been vast. It can be said that Suzie is an evolved person who understands the complexity of human behavior on various levels. None of this, surprisingly, appears to register with Suzie.

Although outwardly Suzie is both adept and extremely personable, nothing makes her feel special. It needs to be emphasized that it has taken me many years and a number of enactments to help me fully appreciate the magnitude to which this is true for her. The discrepancy between how I (and many other people) perceive her and how poorly she has viewed herself has always been quite shocking to me.

Between Suzie's first telephone call to me and the end of her first actual face-to-face session, a number of enactments had taken place that set the scene for the analysis that followed. Suzie telephoned, identified herself by name, and told me a colleague from another city referred her to me. I was sure I knew her name, but could not place her. I imagined she was a colleague, but she did not say that and I did not ask. The day of the appointment Suzie showed up at my office door. Though my door was unlocked, it was new and a bit sticky. Suzie pushed, but not that hard and could not open it. I waited for her in my office not knowing she was on the other side trying to get in. She did not knock, nor call. After a few minutes Suzie left assuming that either I had not remembered the appointment or something must have happened in the interim. The fact (or fantasy) that I was not there, however, did not seem to discourage her. Later that afternoon, she called to make another appointment. I explained that I had been there but had not heard her trying to get in. What a metaphor!

We both took the incident in stride. Those moments do happen. Did it have meaning beyond the surface? We probably both wondered, but filed it aside to begin. We set up another appointment for the next day.

During her first session, Suzie told me she and her husband had just moved to California from London and before that they were living in New York where she was seeing an analyst once a week in psychotherapy. She told me how unsettling everything was: newly married, third city in two years. Not working was especially hard, she said. Not knowing what she could do was even harder. As she began to tell me about her past work, I asked her some questions. Her factual responses left me feeling enormously embarrassed of my questions. I should have known who she was, who she is. In fact, I did. I should have recognized her face. I should have put it together with her familiar sounding name. The only thing I could say was, "Of course. Yes, of course. I was aware of that." I wondered to myself how she felt not to be recognized. Ironically, I believe by not being aware of who she was, I unconsciously resonated with her view of herself, which left her feeling comfortable with me. In her mind, she was not, nor ever has been important to anybody. Why would I know her?

As she began to tell me more about herself, I learned about her pain, her sense of failure and humiliation. The fact that I did not know or recognize her must have also been reassuring to her. It must have meant that I had no preconceived view of who she was. I still do not know why I experienced that lapse. Partially, I believe there was something in her introduction, the way she told me her name that must have quietly alerted me to her own belief that she was not memorable. I would like to presume it is what Chasseguet-Smirgell (1989) calls the maternal aptitude in all analysts. "This hidden thread of mysterious communication ... " (p. 170) that allows the analyst–mother to identify and respond to the preverbal and subverbal aspects of the patient–child. Freud (1915) wrote about those moments, those inexplicable kinds of unconscious-to-unconscious communications that we all have experienced that allow us to know, without words, the state of our patient.

What I am describing with Suzie has also happened with several of my other female patients who also have had no expectations that I will know them, nor that I will want to know them, nor that I will even find them interesting. What made it different with Suzie is that almost immediately this conscious or unconscious belief manifested itself in a concrete manner that allowed me direct access into what I consider the most fundamental aspect of her inner experience—the reason underlying why she was there to see me. Our initial contact/no contact/contact was itself an enactment of something essential and had a profound impact on me personally.

Suzie told me she was particularly interested in seeing a woman therapist. The reasons were hazy, but there was something about the female experience she wanted to know about. She was one of five daughters who, for the most part, were treated as if they were a unit. Each, however, had her role. Together they made one full person. One sister was the beauty; another sister the artist; another was the disturbed one. Suzie was the brain and the athlete. Still another was the drama queen in the family. As the youngest daughter, Suzie was always conflicted about herself as a woman, believing her parents meant for her to be the son they never had. Though she knew she was a girl, she appeared to oblige the family wish by mowing the lawn, washing the cars, working with her father in his tool room, finding ways to obscure her own femininity.

Within the first few sessions Suzie told me that she knew that she needed help. She explained that for almost two decades she suffered silently and privately with bulimia. Recently Suzie admitted to her mother that she had been bulimic. Her mother barely responded and never broached the topic again. One day her husband discovered her secret. Because of his concern, but also his disapproval, she stopped. Suzie emphasized that she knew she had only given up the symptoms, but she was sure the underlying reasons were still there. We discussed the possibility of analysis, not only because of the bulimia, but because Suzie was in pain. She had lost her confidence and was unable to forgive herself for failures that were not altogether her own doing. She was unable to allow her solid accomplishments and her unusual achievement to mitigate her view of herself or her future.

Suzie had a mixed reaction to analysis. She was not surprised I suggested it, though she seemed concerned. Suzie told me her other therapist, an analyst, also thought she would be a good candidate. She was sure that meant we both thought she was crazy. In fact, she thought she was. Feeling crazy is a common experience shared by many of my patients who have been neglected/not known by their kind parents.

The five-day a week analysis began. Treating Suzie created its own complications. I would turn on my television and there she was, talking about issues that were important to her. Yet, she never mentioned during her sessions that she would be on TV. At first, I did not know what to make of it, whether I should bring it up to her or just wait until she did. There is a lot about our patients we may never know about, but that is how it remains. We cannot know what we do not have access to. As time went on, I felt I had to acknowledge my seeing her, because it continued to have a meaning to me that was completely mysterious, and because of that, was often very present when I was in the room with her. These moments that I witnessed were both so public and so private—all at the same time. I felt like a voyeur.

When I finally mentioned to Suzie that I had seen her several times on television, I asked her if there were any conscious reasons why she had not mentioned her appearances. I wondered out loud whether she was just so accustomed to them that they brought up no anxiety for her or was it perhaps just the opposite. Her response took me back. Nothing could have been more removed from my own subjective experience.

Suzie said she did not say anything to me, because she did not think I would be interested in knowing, let alone seeing her. At first I found her explanation difficult to grasp. How could she believe I would not be interested? In fact, if anything I felt guilty because I appeared too fascinated. I know some colleagues will believe that my feelings were intense, because Suzie, unable to bear them herself, projected them into me. Certainly, I held that up as a hypothesis, but the better I began to know her, the more I learned how her belief fit into her life story.

Suzie was a champion soccer player, but no one in her family ever discussed the goals she made. She was also a track star. Though her parents drove her to each practice and often stayed, no one at home ever knew her best time. She was a straight A student with no one there to applaud. She accomplished amazing feats (my belief) and she also had discouraging setbacks. Throughout her life, Suzie did it all alone without either the pleasure of praise and admiration or someone being there to help mitigate the pain of defeat.

The opening phase of analysis proceeded like many others. Our relationship developed. Much time was spent on a peculiar symptom of hers. Suzie would repeatedly lose her wallet, which she carried without a purse. It would almost always be found and returned to her often with the contents in it. Through our work, we began to see it as a reflection of her difficulty holding onto and valuing herself as a metaphor for the treatment. The lack of a purse seemed to represent her conflict over her own self as a female. As the analysis progressed, that particular symptom completely disappeared.

Suzie, during the early phase of treatment, became more focused on her wish to have a family. She suffered a number of painful miscarriages, which were exacerbated by her getting older. At the same time, Suzie's life situation changed. She began making more frequent out-of-state appearances, which required considerable traveling. However, Suzie knew she did not want her work to take control of her as it had in the past, when she ceased having a life of her own. She appreciated the analysis for helping her keep her eye on the prize, that is, being able to stay more present for herself, her wishes and her needs.

During this time, I began to notice something interesting. When Suzie would travel, her absences seemed to disrupt me more than her. She also seemed untouched by my traveling or absences. Initially, I believed she must be repressing her dependency longings. Certainly, that was a possibility. However, interpretations did not make them accessible. What registered to Suzie instead was the fact that I believed she had conflicts surrounding dependency. Occasionally, she would get annoyed with me for making interpretations that she felt were far from her actual experience. Then she would get annoyed with analysis. She would say if it is unconscious, how could you know it, so how could you disprove it? Analysis to her was not a science. She would get frustrated as well that we were talking about her, the patient's subjectivity. However, she would add, I, the analyst, could not help but see it through my own subjectivity. Part of me admired her ability to formulate such cogent critiques of our profession. I was sure she had not read Grunbaum (1984) or Renik (1993). The issue of dependency was always in the air (because it was an assumption I made), but effectively we were unable to work with it.

During the summer, both Suzie and I were absent quite a bit at different times. When our traveling ended and Suzie returned from summer vacation, she informed me emphatically that she was no longer coming five days a week. Suzie told me she knew I would think it was because of her dependency issues or separation issues, but no matter what it was about, her mind was made up. I stated the obvious that she clearly had feelings about the breaks. She said her feelings were that she was happy not to come every day. I wondered out loud if she might have felt abandoned by me. If that is true, she said, it is so far removed from her subjective experience as to render it useless.

Maybe she was angry with me, I suggested. Suzie said she was feeling angry with me, but it was because I was not listening to her. The reality was, she added, she was doing quite well. I remarked being able to function in the outside world has never been her issue. In fact, I said, she has always been an independent person and capable of operating at the highest of levels. That has never been in doubt. However, we both knew it has often been at a cost to her self. She told me that may very well be, but she was not going to let me talk her out of her decision. I knew Suzie was serious. In fact, I had never seen her so insistent with me.

I was not going to try to dissuade her, nor did I want to. That was not my purpose. We were truly engaged with each other in a way we had never been. The feeling in the consulting room was intense. At this point, not knowing exactly what to do, I remembered having a similar situation when I was a candidate in training at the institute with a patient who reminded me very much of Suzie. Both had comparable family dynamics. Their transferences to me were similar as was my countertransference to them. Because I was in supervision at that time, I found myself constantly making interpretations dealing with how many days of the week she came and what it meant (Zalusky, 1995). In reality, I was never comfortable making my patient conform to a structure she did not want. The only thing I did know for sure was that I was not going to do the same with Suzie. I had no intention of interpreting her into a treatment plan to which she objected, even if her objections turned out to be her defense against intimacy. I told Suzie that I completely understood that she was not coming five days a week. I added we both knew that her highly defended self worked to keep her feeling self away. I told her I believed her coming five days a week kept her more connected with me but also more importantly with herself. Though I was aware that she was not going to continue with the analysis the way it had been, it did not change my mind about what I thought was helpful. Knowing her made me believe the frequency of sessions helped both of us to become acquainted with her more vulnerable side. Yet, at the moment she appeared obviously to prefer her more impenetrable self.

It was nearing the end of the session. Not knowing what to do, I asked her what she had in mind. She said she did not know. I asked her when would I see her next. Suzie thought for a second and said, "Not tomorrow, but Wednesday." That became our ritual for the next year and a half. At the end of each session I would ask her when she would be coming back. Some weeks she came three times a week, others twice a week, sometimes four times, frequently five times a week, and occasionally once a week. Sometimes she would use the couch, sometimes not. Unless it was completely obvious why she was not coming on a particular day, I chose not to interpret it nor to explore it. I let Suzie be in charge of that aspect of her treatment. We were both co-constructing the structure, but whether this would be a successful compromise, neither one of us knew. We were creating something new as we were going along.

At first I had no theory on which to base our moves. The only thing I could rely on was my "motherly" instinct to help guide us to a suitable arrangement that both of us could endure, which would allow the analysis to continue in some form. When I was able, I kept her original appointment times available. However, if I needed to change them, I would. The variations in our hours met with no apparent objection from Suzie. She accepted the changes as part of the compromises we were both making. Initially, however, the traditional analyst in me felt guilty for agreeing to a plan that was so unorthodox. Because of this, I called one of my institute's most conservative analysts, my analytic superego, to consult with him. He told me that he knew himself well enough to know that he could never agree to such a plan. It would make him angry. He liked to know his schedule; how much he was earning, and the like. But he gave me "his permission." If I wanted to experiment, why not do so. Oddly, I never felt angry with Suzie or with our agreement. It did not feel like she was doing something to me personally.

Within the first few weeks of our changed schedule, Suzie accused me of being controlling. I was taken aback. I told her, "I'm surprised. In fact, with our new treatment plan I never felt less controlling in my life." She explained that by holding onto my idea of what was best for her, even though I was going along with her, I was still attempting to influence her. Therefore, I was trying to control her. Certainly, I knew that partly she was right. Her view gave us the space to analyze what it means to hold onto one's ideas, what it means to be influenced and how the two were linked in her mind. Up until then, her career had been about delivering other people's ideas. She did it so well, that she began to confuse her ideas with the ideas she was espousing. It was a new experience for her to see me hold onto my beliefs, yet adapt to what she wanted or needed. As I adapted, interestingly enough, I changed too. I began to question my own beliefs. Maybe she really did know what she needed.

I noticed many of my patients who had disappearing (or ghost) mothers, consistently vanished from me. I could not help but wonder why that was. Suzie never disappeared without letting me know first that she would not be there. Yet, many of my less-functioning patients leave me never knowing whether they are going to come to session or not. The transference implication is much clearer with them. Unconsciously, they let me feel what their experience has been. It's been patchy. The people they relied on were intermittently not present when they expected them to be there. They never knew when their caregivers might physically or emotionally return. I found the same to be true with these patients. They disappear, but they do return. Sometimes they are emotionally available and other times they are not.

I have also learned from my patients, often from their dreams, that having me consistently there, day in and day out, can feel quite overwhelming, engulfing, especially when one is not used to that type of involvement with another person. To preserve themselves, they often feel the need to cut off communication. As analysts, we hope that by interpreting these phenomena, the behavior will be transformed. These feelings are often so fundamental, so deep, that words do not seem to touch these patients—for these patients' actions often speak much louder than words.

With Suzie the work of analysis continued. But it was feeding on demand, not on schedule. When she needed me, I was there. When it felt burdensome, she could make me disappear for a day or two, until she wanted to see me again and I would be there. At times, she wanted to see me, but her job would keep her away. Most of this went unsaid. It was the background, the texture of the analysis.

We analysts think four or five days a week is a better holding environment and for some it is even necessary. However, for others it is too much too soon. It is hard to make the analyst that important when nobody has ever made them feel important enough. I believe even more essential, it is also hard to let someone else know that they have meaning to you when you do not believe you have meaning to them. Sadly, many of our patients are convinced they have no meaning to us.

At some point, Suzie asked to have regularly scheduled appointments again. She wanted to have both the consistency of the appointments and a schedule. It was now she who created for herself a five-day-a-week analysis with an analyst who was somewhat in her control. As Winnicott (1969) said, first the object needs to be found before she can be used. Suzie was beginning to find me, to know that I was reliably there, even if she did not believe she mattered to me. Obviously, her issues did not magically go away, but they were now available for us to work with. During this time, Suzie became pregnant. Something had shifted in our relationship that allowed Suzie to be open to a more consistent way of relating to me, her analyst. It is impossible to know how this new desire to relate had affected her ability to maintain a pregnancy, however, we do know it gave her an opportunity to explore her own conflicts around being a mother and being mothered (Zalusky, 2000).

Suzie wanted help becoming a mother who was capable of being present for her child. During the early part of her pregnancy, Suzie had a dream in which she forgot to feed her baby. Ironically, many of my patients with disappearing mothers dream during pregnancy of forgetting to nourish their children. The dream naturally disturbed her. She worried about her own ability to stay present. She felt her husband would make a much better nurturing mother than she could. Her belief made her sad. She wanted to be that mother who could nurture her child in every way possible.

Through our work, it became more obvious that she wanted to be known by me, a mother figure that could help her know about herself as a woman and create for herself a mother who was emotionally there. At the same time while we were analyzing her fears related to mothering, one of her sisters became very ill. She immediately, if not instinctively, took care of her. Her parents did not let the magnitude of their daughter's illness register. They did not fly in once to visit. Though I was surprised at their absence, Suzie was not. Neither was her sister. The subject of their parents' nonappearance was not spoken between them. No one expected them to be there, so they disappointed no one.

Next, a series of events happened that changed the nature of the analysis. Ironically, sometime in Suzie's ninth month, the doctors became alarmed, believing Suzie's placenta no longer was nourishing her baby. I received a call from her husband saying that Suzie would have to miss her session. The doctors were about to induce labor. The next day I received a call again from Suzie's jubilant husband telling me that they had a beautiful, healthy baby boy and that mother and child were doing well. I left a message of congratulations, but I never heard directly from my patient. I began to feel terrible. What did that mean about our relationship that she did not call me? Was I so unimportant to her, so removed from her life? Was she afraid I could not tolerate her being a mother? Clearly, she was regressing to an earlier level of relating, at least in relationship to me, her analyst. I felt conflicted about what I should do. On the one hand, I did not want to intrude if she desired space. On the other hand, I did not want to recreate old familial patterns of disappearing during important moments. I waited three weeks and then called. I was a bit surprised to hear how happy she was to talk to me. As always, I asked her when she would be coming back. She said, "Not too soon. Let's wait until next week."

For years we have used the birth of her first born as a template for her experience with me, elaborating on it time and time again. Initially, I asked Suzie why she had not telephoned me personally. She told me she heard her husband calling me both times. I asked why him and not her. She said when she heard him calling, she wondered the same, why was he making the call, but she did not say anything to him. Suzie began to notice how easily she allowed her own experience to be usurped. It was something she had always done and in the past had been greatly rewarded for it. The result, she discovered, was she stopped paying attention to her own feelings, until she barely noticed her own reactions, and when she did, she often dismissed them. We were able to link this to her life-long struggle with bulimia.

Beyond the suppression of her own experience, Suzie surprised me again. At another time I asked her even though she heard her husband call me, why did she not call me later herself or take the phone. Suzie astounded me when she said her husband had already told me they had a new baby and she did not call personally because she did not want to bother me again. The notion that I, her analyst–mother, would care because I cared was still so removed from her experience. Even at her most celebrated moment, rather than appreciating it with her, she expected me to experience her as a burden. She quietly obliged her fantasy and disappeared to take care of herself and her new baby.

As years went on and Suzie elaborated on what it meant not to call me, I began to fill in what it meant to me that she did not call. Suzie was fascinated that my feelings were hurt at the time, that she could hurt them. She began to realize that I could be interested in both her inner and outer life. It was not that she could not appreciate me as a separate person, because she did. At first I was a separate person who could hold only a very small place in my mind for her and only during her appointments. As time went on, she was able to amplify the type and depth of experiences a mother–analyst–person could have for a child–patient–person.

During this time, another sister who was six months pregnant was on a business trip. She was in a serious car accident and prematurely began labor. The doctors were convinced that her child would not be able to survive delivery. Suzie, knowing that she could arrive sooner than her sister's husband could, took a plane to be there for her sister when she woke up. Suzie was full of sadness, full of tears. Intellectually, she understood her sister would need someone close. Suzie also believed her sister would not know that she would need someone to be there for her, to care about her emotional reactions, to help her deal with her mourning. Suzie knew she would need someone. Nonetheless, it was still an emotional risk for her to take. She was dealing with two conflicting voices. One voice, the familiar one, wondered whether she would really be needed. After all, Suzie would be fulfilling a role that virtually was unknown to any of the members of her family. The other voice, though quiet and still not fully developed, knew she wanted to be there for her sister and she was.

After many years, what is most noticeable is that Suzie has constructed a place in her mind that holds me as someone who cares about her, who cares to remember her when she is not there. We both are able to acknowledge the importance of her accomplishment and the ramifications both of not having an available internal mother and of having one. It is not as easy for either one of us to fade for any period of time now without it being noticed. There will always be the internal representations of a disappearing mother, but beside her now lives another mother who is available, who cares and wants to be present. This side of her personality is becoming increasingly stronger. Obviously, it affects the analysis. There is a qualitative difference in how Suzie communicates with me. There appears to be a shared loving feeling, which allows her to deal more openly with intimate feelings.

Suzie has been adjusting to a new "reality," where caring and feeling create their own complications. Suzie is an involved and interested mother. She enjoys thinking about her children. She now has three. She takes pleasure in playing with each child, being there for each one individually and wondering what each is experiencing. She has made almost every career choice in relation to what it would mean to her children's development. She's there to take them to school and to tuck them in at night. If she needs to travel, Suzie tries to leave on the red eye and to return home as soon as possible, even if it requires her missing something she otherwise wished she could attend. She works out of the house so if her children need her, she is around. Naturally, Suzie deals with the compromises she has made in regard to her career. It is a much smaller career than it started off being, and she is conflicted about that. She is trying and has, to a great degree, found her own voice, which could affect how she develops her options for the future. Outside people in her field who she values and admires have remarked to her recently that she appears to be a centered and healthy person.

Her relationship with her husband has also been in an adjustment phase. Suzie expects more availability from him than she used to, although she is beginning to recognize her own part in his behavior. She is changing their unspoken contract in mid-stream and he is having difficulty at times shifting his focus. Suzie also wants him to pay more attention to their children, which we both understand to mean the real ones and the child inside of her.

Recently Suzie had a dream before giving birth to her third baby. In the dream, she was with her mother and forgot to take the baby home from the hospital. Suzie began to panic, worrying who was going to feed the baby.

She told her mother she needed to get back to the baby to nourish her. The mother told her not to worry—that it wasn't important. At first, she listens to her mother, but her worry about the baby overrides her mother's nonchalance. She goes back and brings the baby home with her. She hears the baby's cry and provides for her. In working on the dream, we both recognized Suzie's personal development and its impact on her ability to mother.

Schwartz (1993) describes three categories of mothering functions, which are all central to the mothering relation: security, regulation, and recognition. Disturbances in recognition, she and others suggest, may have serious consequences in the woman's ability to develop healthy narcissism, which ultimately affects all relationships. This deficit, if not attended, most often is passed down through the generations.

Analysis helped Suzie to find and recognize the need for an available mother within. With recognition came the wish to be the available mother to her own children. Suzie, in finding her own nurturing mother, found her own children. By mothering her children in the flesh and blood, she opened up the possibility of returning to the lonely neglected child within, which allowed her to continue her own process of healing.

Discussion

Initially, Freud made the assumption that analysis requires the patient's emotional engagement with the analyst–therapist, but with many of our patients, our work consists of creating just that. We need to help our patients develop the capacity to have meaningful intimate affectionate relationships. Natterson (2003) believes all therapy is about the unleashing of the potential for love. He suggests that "Love is a fundamental dynamic element of the therapeutic process itself, as it is of all creative, intimate relationships" (p. 509). He believes, along with Lear (1990), that love and self are "inseparable and that the unfolding of one entails the strengthening of the other" (p. 510). The question, however, remains: how do we unlock the potential for love in patients who do not have confidence in their basic lovability?

The patients I have described in this article, who tend to present with a disappearing (or ghost) mother transference, often do not let us work in the fashion to which we have grown accustomed. I believe they force us to adapt to them, because that is a necessary precondition for them to begin to know that we care (Hoffman, 1994), that we see them. The way we adapt must be specific to the specific patient, to their specific implicit or explicit demands, and to our own temperament (i.e., what is acceptable to us, not necessarily our theory).

For some patients, we need to find them, to search them out, before they can use us (Winnicott, 1971/1999). For others like Suzie, they need to find us. The treatment of certain types of patients requires that the analyst not have a one-size-fits-all type of practice. Patients do have diverse histories and different expressions of long-standing problems, some of which require an adjustment in our technique. If we cannot do that, we probably cannot help them without creating a situation in which they submit to our need in order to be helped.

At the time, I had no explicit rationale for going along with Suzie's plan other than an intuitive understanding that Suzie could not continue if she did not feel more in control of her coming and goings. In retrospect, I believed we needed to co-create a space, similar to what Winnicott (1971/1999) discussed in his article on transitional objects and transitional phenomena. In this article, Winnicott explained the importance to the psychological development of the infant that he has the illusion of creating the breast when it appears. Winnicott suggested that it is through the baby's need and the adaptation to his need that love develops. By not questioning or interpreting to Suzie the meaning of her comings and goings, I, albeit unconsciously, allowed Suzie to create over and over again her own analyst and analysis. Winnicott believes the illusion of the baby creating the breast is the basis for the infant's initiation of experience. It is a neutral area, which should not be challenged. He states, " ... *it can be said that it is a matter of agreement between us and the baby that we will never ask the question: 'Did you conceive of this or was it presented to you from without?' The important point is that no decision on this point is expected. The question is not to be formulated*" (Italics the author's, not mine, p. 12).

I believe this is partly why these kinds of patients need to disappear. If we are always there, it is not they who create us. Another patient of mine, who has had the most incredible history of loss and family illness, began treatment by never showing up. The colleague who referred her to me warned me of this, but added she does pay her bills. In actuality, it was her parents who paid her bills. Her three weekly appointments stayed the same week after week, whether she was there or not. For her, we played a game of hide and seek. I needed to look for her and to wonder where she was, before she could eventually let me find her. After some period of time, to let me know she had not forgotten about me or her treatment, she would intermittently call to explain that though she had slept through her session (at 3:00 pm, 9:00 am, 12:30 pm, 6:00 pm, whenever), she hoped to be at our next scheduled one. When she did not show up, I would call her, trying to find her. As the treatment proceeded and she was more connected to me, she would telephone in advance to let me know apologetically that she would not be able to be there later in the day. At times, I could not help but become annoyed with her, and then she would appear at the next session to make sure I would still be there. When she would come, she would always be sweet and always engaging. As things progressed, she might come for half a session, then almost a whole session. She created her own version of peek-a-boo. Then she would miss once again. Or she would come for the last five minutes of her appointment. As the work deepened, she would disappear again for a period of time. After a serious crisis in which we contemplated hospitalization, we decided to increase her sessions to five days a week. In the last year, she has made almost every session and is currently coming on time. In one of her most recent appearances she said to me jokingly, "I worked hard to get you to love me." I asked her why she needed to work so hard. She said, "You are right. I am very loveable you know." I agreed, but added, "Maybe one day you will really know that too." By making me love her, which was her illusion, because I already did, she created a space inside of her where I continued to care for her, even when she was unable to do so. Now she is beginning to struggle in the present both with the future as well as with her painful past. She is also allowing herself to become more irritable and annoyed with me, which I see as progress.

Gabbard and Westin (2003) indicate in their article "Rethinking Therapeutic Action" that we must stop asking whether something is analytic, but rather if is it therapeutic. Reviewing the literature on therapeutic action, they rightfully conclude there is not one type of therapeutic action, but many.

There are numerous factors that contributed to Suzie's being able to use our work differently. Although I emphasized in this article the relational aspects of our work, it was because the relational facilitated Suzie being able to use my interpretation to gain insight and then to teach me more about her and my understanding of her. I have not given up my traditional analytic ideas concerning conflicts and defenses against dependency, sexuality, and aggression, but sometimes, I believe ghost mother–analysts need their patients to turn them into real warm-blooded people before they can take advantage of our more traditional offerings. Dependency needs to develop before it can be interpreted.

REFERENCES

Chasseguet-Smirgell, J. (1989), The femininity of the analyst in professional practice, *International Journal of Psychoanalysis,* 65: 169–178.

Freud, S. (1915), The unconscious. *Standard Edition* 14: 1957, London: Hogarth Press, 159–215.

Gabbard, G. (1999), On gratitude and gratification. Plenary address presented at American Psychoanalytic Association, May, Washington, DC.

_____ & Westin, D. (2003), Rethinking therapeutic action, *Int. J. Psycho-Anal.* 84: 823–841.

Grunbaum, A. (1984), *The Foundations of Psychoanalysis.* Berkely: University of California Press.

Hoffman, I. Z. (1994), Dialectical thinking and therapeutic action in the psychoanalytic process, *Psychoanal. Quart.,* 63:187–218.

Lear, J. (1990), *Love and Its Place in Nature.* New York: Farrar, Straus and Giroux.

Natterson, J. (2003), Love in Psychotherapy, *Psychoanal. Psychol.,* 20:3509–521.

Renik, O. (1993), Conceptualizing technique in light of the analyst's irreducible subjectivity, *Psychoanal. Quart.,* Vol. 62:551–571.

_____ (1994), Publication of clinical facts, *Internat. J. Psycho-Anal.,* 75:1245–1250.

_____ (1998), The analyst's subjectivity and the analyst's objectivity, *Internat. J. Psycho-Anal.,* 79:487–497

Schwartz, A. E. (1993), Thoughts on the constructions of maternal representations, *Psychoanal. Psychol.,* 10:331–344.

Winnicott, D. W. (1969), The use of the object, *International Journal of Psychoanalysis,* 50:711–716.

_____ (1971/1999), *Transitional Objects and Transitional Phenomena in Playing and Reality.* London: Routledge, pp. 1–25.

Zalusky, S. (1995), Analyzability from an intersubjective perspective. Unpublished doctoral thesis, Southern California Psychoanalytic Institute.

_____ (2000). Infertility in the age of technology, *J. Amer. Pyschoanal. Assn.,* 48:1541–1562.

11980 San Vicente Blvd. #904
Los Angeles, CA 90049
szalusky@aol.com

Mothers and Daughters as Adults

MALKAH T. NOTMAN, M.D.

For most women, their relationship with their mothers, both external and internal, remains important throughout life, although it may be intensely ambivalent. The tension between the ongoing process of differentiation and developing a sense of self, and also maintaining the attachments that have been present during development into adulthood, continue to be present, fluctuating with life events and changes for both daughters and mothers. The body with its similarities to the mother, mutual identification, and competitive aspects is a central area for experiencing this relationship. A patient who illustrates these processes is described.

IN MOZART'S OPERA *THE MAGIC FLUTE,* THE QUEEN OF THE NIGHT FIRST appears as a distraught mother whose daughter has been abducted by Sarastro, described by her as a wicked sorcerer. She enlists the help of the prince, Tamino, to rescue her daughter, Pamina. She has the magic flute given to him to help him in his search. In Act II she is no longer the abandoned sad mother but appears as a wicked witch. Sarastro is portrayed as a kind, responsible protector. That transformation of the Queen of the Night had always puzzled me. When Sarastro appears on the scene he too is different than one expects. He turns out to be powerful but although there was an abduction, it is not he but his servant who is sexually interested in Pamina. He protects her but says she must be freed from her mother who has "too much pride" and she must also be freed by a prince. So he is a good father. How can one reconcile this additional contradiction?

Malkah T. Notman, M.D. is a Clinical Professor of Psychiatry, Harvard Medical School and Director of Faculty Development, Cambridge Health Alliance, and is the author of several books, including, most recently, Bloom, J., Nadelson, C., and Notman, M. (eds) *Physician Sexual Misconduct.* APPI, 1999.

There are some disparaging remarks about women and their rationality, but one can look beyond these. The story can be understood as a developmental tale for Pamina in her relationship with her mother. One realizes that it is only through the Queen's eyes that Sarastro is seen and then portrayed as the villain. As the good father, he helps the daughter separate from her mother. He saves her for the prince, who must also grow up by proving himself. Pamina is also saved by the abduction from owning the aggression and sexuality that the separation involved. One can explain that the Queen of the Night turns wicked so Pamina can detach herself. She cannot carry out her mother's murderous instructions, so she also develops her own voice. Her aggression is projected onto her mother, the wicked one. In Act II toward the end, when the prince and Pamina are reunited, Pamina gives him back the magic flute. Only then does she tell him that it was made by her father. So he now has the blessing from her father as well in the form of the magic phallic object.

In *The Magic Flute,* the Queen of the Night is transformed and demonized, so Pamina with the support of the man, can leave her. In real life, this is a much slower process than in opera and not so straightforward. Separation and individuation takes a while and doesn't happen with such finality. It is a lifelong task and colors adult as well as adolescent mother–daughter relationships. So one of the ongoing developmental issues for women is the tension between attachment to one's mother and developing some autonomy.

The myth of Persephone has also been explained by Kulish and Holtzman (1998) and Holtzman and Kulish (2000) as a model for the girl's development. Persephone is abducted by Hades, to the distress of Demeter, her mother, the Goddess of Grain, who comes to earth to search for her. In her distress, Demeter creates drought and barrenness on earth. In the final negotiation among the gods, Persephone is allowed to come back to earth for six months, and, because she has eaten some forbidden pomegranate seeds in the underworld, she must return to the underworld for six months each year. Holtzman and Kulish use this myth as a description of the female triangular situation—when the girl's entry into heterosexuality is also portrayed as an abduction, not as her willing separation from her mother.

Bernstein (2004, p. 615) describes it as a "tale of divided loyalties," closeness with the mother disrupted by a sexual drive. Unlike *The Magic Flute,* the separation is not permanent, and the Persephone myth also emphasizes the power of the mother. The Queen of the Night violently disappears after her murderous plan is frustrated. Demeter's sadness has a profound effect on the earth. The Persephone myth also brings up the mother's need to deal with the loss of her daughter in the normal course of events as she grows up and makes her new attachments.

The potential loss of the daughter to another person—husband or lover—is another source of problems for her mother. The mother can feel reluctant to give up possession of her daughter to a stranger. It is not clear whether it is more threatening to lose a daughter to a man or to a woman. In the Persephone myth she does not lose her daughter forever. This is closer to real life.

Freud, in *Totem and Taboo,* discusses the relationship between the son-in-law and the mother-in-law. He described that the mother-in-law, in her identification with her daughter, "can fall in love with the man her daughter loves" (Freud, 1913, p. 15). Then she can avoid the loss and also disappointments if her own marriage has become "emotionally uneventful."

What do we know, clinically, about the adult mother–daughter relationship? With many individual variations, it remains a highly important relationship. Throughout life, the power of this relationship persists, even when the daughter may be independent, geographically separate, in her own family, or alone. This does not mean it is regressive. It is not always loving or close.

Bernstein (2004), in an excellent review of mothers and daughters from today's psychoanalytic perspective, described Freud's and other earlier views of the girl's development that held that development is linear and the attachment and connectedness with the mother is an indication of regression or failure of separation. She emphasized that "the daughter's involvement with her 'inner and outer mother' is not regressive in the pojorative sense." She refers to Dahl (1995), and writes "There is a constant process of reworking 'self vs mother and self-with mother' representations" (Bernstein, 2004, p. 622).

That the mother in adulthood remains an important source of conflicts but also attachments may be surprising to a daughter who sees herself as independent, strong, resourceful, and mature.

T, a successful business woman, lost her mother when she was 10 years old. She had several older sisters and a difficult, physically abusive father who, however, emphasized achievement, which she felt was for his own glory. She moved back to New England and reconnected with some old friends and their families. Seeing these families anew she said she began to fully realize how different her own life had been. She said, "The importance of mothers in adult women's lives on a consistent basis is now really clear to me—for support and just a whole lot of different things." She has been independent and successful and not unaware of her feelings of loss and sadness about not having had a mother but had not been so aware of the many ways this made an immense difference in her life.

P, a 54-year old woman, had experienced many moves as a child. It was clear that her interests and wishes were less important than parental professional agendas and were often disregarded. She was impressed that she is still looking for a place "in her mother's view," and hears her mother's statements over and over in a way that appears to her to be excluding her yet again. It is painful each time.

J's mother, a woman with a long history of severe depressive episodes, reacted to her daughter's announcement about her third pregnancy with anger, leaving her 40-year-old daughter confused and upset. The mother's hostility had a variety of sources, which her daughter understood, but the effect was an intense feeling of rejection and dismay.

So one of the recurrent themes in the psychoanalytic understanding of adult mother–daughter relationships has to do with the conflict between the daughter's attachment and dependency on the mother and her need to develop her individuality and autonomy. This remains a lifelong process. In adulthood, there is also a continuation from childhood and adolescence of negotiation of the old conflicts: ambivalence, the tension between separation–individuation and attachment, and sensitivity to loss and separation. Some change in the daughter's life that creates a shift in differentiation can change the manifest tone in the relationship.

Tension can remain diffuse and simmering, to flare up at what appear like minor provocations, with hostility directed at the mother who is blamed for failures or for perceived injuries.

In a recent small series of interviews of mothers with adult daughters, a number of women described tensions between themselves and their adult daughters that had been present at least since adolescence. These had a number of different sources. For some, there was unresolved resentment from the birth of siblings, competitive feelings or envy of siblings, or feeling that the daughter was always secondary to someone else. Sometimes there were overt confrontations; at other times, there was a readiness to get into fights over small differences. Each mother described a change that took place in her relationship that followed a shift in the daughter's life. One daughter developed a stable relationship with a man.

The tension with her mother eased; they talked more, and she included her mother in details about her life. This change remained even though the relationship with the man did not last. Another described a similar change when the daughter married. It appeared not to be connected with the economic or social status of the marriage, but with having the man, a man of her own. It placed her in an equal position to her mother and gave her a position of her own. Another daughter found a place with success in work—a specific promotion. It appeared that some stability and resolution could be achieved with her mother with the development of her own feelings of differentiation and equality. Work can provide a competitive arena that can contribute to a sense of self. One is a person in one's own right. Marriage can accomplish some of the same separation and consequent shift in the relationship. The separation does not have to be reinforced by ongoing distancing tension.

The tie to the mother can be experienced as imprisoning; aggression toward her may need to be denied, displaced, or experienced as competition, rivalry, or envy. Conflicts over aggression play a lifelong role. For the mother, envy, rivalry, identification, and pleasure in a daughter's flowering and success can be accompanied by envy of her youth, future possibilities, sexuality, and fertility.

The mother can experience her menopause in many ways. One possibility is as a time of potential freedom, with new energy and direction, but it also emphasizes that she gives up the possibility of pregnancy and is a herald to aging. Whether or not she consciously wishes for another pregnancy, she can feel envy and competition at the daughter's possible childbearing.

G, in her 40's, was enthusiastically preparing for her daughter's wedding. During the ceremony, as she was walking down the aisle with her daughter, she felt nauseous, and realized she herself was pregnant, which she had not consciously intended.

The mother can also envy the daughter's actual resources and choices, particularly if they appear to offer more than the mother has or had.

H, in her 50's, had experienced parental separation and poverty growing up. She had been eager to have children and give them a better life than she had. She had two daughters, both accomplished and beautiful. The younger one married first, a wealthy man from a stable family with a good career. Pleased as she was, she found herself angry at her daughter's luxurious home and swimming pool and all the fancy kitchen appliances that she had never had.

The mother may look to her daughter for the realization of her own fantasies of achievement and success that were not available when she herself was a young adult. The daughter, needing to please her mother, acts as a compliant "good girl," although this may involve aggressive career pursuit.

The rapid social changes within the past generation can create some particular dilemmas between mothers and daughters that are analogous to the conflicts between parents of an immigrant generation and their children. The daughters can experience conflict between identification with their mother and new social pressures. Expectations for women to develop careers and to succeed in work have become more commonplace. Some of this change is because of increased opportunities for women, as a result of the women's movement. Some is because of economic pressure, so two jobs in a family are necessary. There is a paradoxical aspect to this change. Women have been described as more likely to conform, to seek approval, to avoid aggressive confrontation more than men, although they are increasingly willing to be assertive and ambitious in some work situations. So the wish to please, to fulfill mothers' fantasies, or to conform to new societal expectations can lead young women to career ambitions that can then stand in the way of the traditional feminine goals of children and family. Some young women then abandon their work goals in the face of family needs or because their investment in these is secondary and childcare is expensive and difficult to arrange. This can also be because the demands of work may not entirely represent their own primary interests or wishes but a wish to do the right thing. Thus, the need to please, or fulfill one's mother's fantasies, and be a "good girl," can bring the young woman into conflict with her mother's expectation for grandchildren or more traditional family life. Work and career can be consistent with expressions of aggression and ambition possibly not openly recognized by her mother. There can thus be internal conflict between identification with her mother and her own ambitions and rebellion. For the daughter, achievement can also represent a source of conflict as a competitive victory, about which she can feel guilty as well as gratified.

Depression is more prevalent in women worldwide. Many reasons for this have been offered. The helplessness accompanying poverty, powerlessness related to social factors, personality factors of passivity, and dependency have been implicated. It is not yet clear what the effects of more women working will be on this greater incidence and prevalence of depression in women. Studies of women and work in this country (Barnett, 2004) document the positive psychological effects of work for women in many ways.

Literature

There is not a great deal of psychoanalytic literature about adult mother–daughter relationships. Psychoanalytic writing appears mostly in clinical accounts except for a few topics, such as pregnancy. Clinical writing is usually from the point of view of one person—often the daughter as the patient. The mother may thus be seen as the mother of childhood, or in a relatively static way, not considering her own developmental changes and experiences or her inner life and the effects on the daughter. The impact on the daughter of the mother's life changes such as divorce, widowhood, and career success are rarely considered in depth in this context.

There are several areas in which there has been more extensive writing. One of these concerns pregnancy. The entrance into motherhood, and the relationship of the daughter and mother during pregnancy, is obviously important (Balsam, 1996). The daughter is transformed from a daughter to a mother but retains her relationship as daughter to her mother. The actual experience of pregnancy was not studied psychoanalytically until the 1950s and 1960s. Freud's theoretical formulations about pregnancy and the meaning of the baby for the mother were developed without examining the experiences of pregnant women. The studies in the 1950s and 1960s by analysts reflected the interests of the women psychoanalysts who initiated them (Bibring, 1959; Jessner, et al., 1970). These studies also reflect the analysts' conceptualization about what is central in a woman's life, not only her reproductive function but also an identity and self-concept in which childbearing is primary.

Bibring (1959, 1961) saw pregnancy, particularly a first pregnancy, as a "developmental crisis," in Eriksonian terms. She thought it to be a period of the potential renegotiation of the mother–daughter relationship. She and the other investigators thought that "in pregnancy, as in puberty and menopause, new and increased libidinal and adjustive tasks confront the individual, leading to the revival and emergence of unsettled conflicts from earlier developmental phases and to the loosening of partial or inadequate solutions of the past" (Bibring, 1959, p. 116). In this process, new and better relationships could be arrived at, including a shift in the identification with the mother.

Pines (1991) saw pregnancy as a developmental phase in a woman's lifelong task of separation–individuation from her own mother. She saw the dual identification for a pregnant woman both with her own mother and the baby inside her.

Hoffman (2004) quotes Dan Stern's concept of the "motherhood constellation," which describes the appearance of a new psychic organization in the new mother, which he believes normalized the new mother's state and took it out of the realm of "inevitable regression," which has been true in prior writing. Bibring (1959, p. 116) actually used the "developmental crisis" concept as a statement of an opportunity for new development. Stern (1995) describes this "motherhood constellation" as involving for the new mother a "discourse with her own mother as well as herself and her baby." In all these writings, the internal relationship of the new mother to her own mother is central. Some feel it is even more important than her relationship to her husband or father.

Bernstein (2004) reviews the literature and current thought about the development of daughters and mothers and believes these fundamental dynamics are brought into adulthood. She emphasizes the ongoing and reciprocal struggles with rivalry, jealousy, and ambivalence. The girl's development is understood to be nonlinear; her attachment to her mother remains and is a "feature of object relations for women that is not in itself pathologic" (Bernstein, 2004, p. 622).

That becoming a parent is transforming was also recognized by Benedek (1970). She wrote about its developmental impact and the parents' continual changes in response to the child's needs and behavior. She did not specifically focus on motherhood or changes in response to adult children. Since then, many articles have addressed the psychology of motherhood, but its absence reflects the psychoanalytic orientation of the 1960s and 1970s.

In the literature on the life cycle and adult development, the succession of life stages is described. However, in this literature as well, there is no specific consideration of mothers and daughters. Erikson (1950) formulated his well-known concepts of developmental stages. He wrote that early adulthood was characterized by the contrast of "intimacy vs. isolation" and later adulthood by " generativity," although it is interesting that he did not refer to pregnancy or reproduction. He wrote about the "relationship of the older generation to the younger one" and "a man's relationship to his production as well as his progeny" and that the "generativity is primarily the concern in establishing and guiding the next generation" (p. 267). He also believed that development goes on throughout life, but he did not specifically refer to mothers and daughters. Jaques (1980), in his work on midlife crisis, used only men as his examples. In their formulations about middle age, Auchinclos and Michels (1989) looked for generalizations about the inner experiences of middle age but did not focus on parents and offspring. They suggested three modalities of the middle years. One view is that the same fantasies are present as in earlier life, with different expressions during the life course. Another position is that new defensive styles and modes of adaptation can emerge in middle age. A third concept is that continued growth leads to changes in the basic components of conflict and fantasy.

How can one understand the shifts in both daughters and mothers in daughters that are adults? Whether they see each other as peers and contemporaries, are intimate and close or distant, residues of old relationships remain.

Benedek (1970a, p. 196) wrote that "with the adult child's marriage the immediate responsibility of parenthood for the child is discontinued ." She described the "emancipation of the daughters from their mothers" because of contemporary social changes. These ideas and the internal psychic realities of the mother and adult daughter do not include what we know about ongoing attachment, identifications, and conflicts. They also reflect the changing nature of marriage.

Shrier, Tompsett, and Shrier (2004) review the theoretical and research literature on adult mother–daughter relationships, drawing from psychoanalytic developmental and other relevant literature with a focus on normative, nonclinical relationships between mothers and their adult daughters. In this review, they also note the dearth of psychoanalytic literature in this area except as extensions of developmental theory. In the extension from ideas of female development, they cite both Chodorow (1978/1999) and the group associated with Jean Baker Miller (1973, p. 95) who emphasize the "maternal identification and mutual reciprocal processes" involved in women's adult relationships, including the mother and adult daughter. As a summary of these writings, they conclude that although "the daughter's relationship with her mother becomes increasingly complex and differentiated … it … is retuned on a lifelong basis and serves as a precursor and template for evolving relationships with others" (p. 111).

Balsam (2003) emphasized the impact of the internalization of the mother for female development and stated that the "internalizations involve a psychological system of projection, introjection, reprojection, and reintrojection of certain unconsciously incorporated and imitated elements of the mother, be they body or mind" (p. 88). These internalizations become particularly available to consciousness when special milestones of a life cycle, such as pregnancy, are repeated by the next generation.

The Body

The girl's early erotic tie to her mother is important in developing her own sensuality. Mothers and daughters share having a female body. The daughter's relationship to the mother's body and the mother's to the daughter's body is an important aspect of the relationship. Bernstein (2004) discusses the girl's erotic attachment and wishes for the mother's body. The girl growing into adulthood assesses herself in relation to the mother's body. Her visual perception, the comparison of the mother's and daughter's shape, including breasts, and her self concept as "feminine" contain the sense of having a similar body as her mother and of being the same to some extent. The mother's response to having a baby girl is thought to contain the awareness of their being "the same," having the same body. The adolescent girl, unlike the boy, develops a new body part—the breasts—that is not evident in childhood. Her breasts, their size, and shape also evoke comparison with her mother.

Identification between mother and daughter is mutual. Bernstein (2004) describes these feelings: "In the body of her infant daughter, a mother can see her own past self; the body is known and familiar, one with which she can have total identification. This is sometimes competitive, sometimes with the sense of oneness. It extends throughout her life through the changes in the body with adolescence and the beginning of menstruation, the growth of the breasts, and later, pregnancy and then menopause." Girls look to their mother's experience with menopause to predict their own menopause even though genetically they may be more like their fathers' families and the women in them. Later, the daughter looks to her mother to see how she will age, and even how she will die. The daughter can have a direct awareness and identification with her mother's body as having contained and produced her.

One teenage pregnant orphaned girl expressed that she felt a strong wish to have seen her mother, "in whose belly I was." Sometimes the bodily feelings are the vehicle for expression of emotional connection.

B, a teacher, had an ambivalent, distant relationship to her mother. She couldn't bear being physically close to her and had resisted hugs and caresses throughout childhood. After her mother recovered from a severe illness, B realized her feelings for her mother were more complicated than she had thought. She described that, while standing in front of her class, she had the feeling that she was "the same flesh" as her mother, that they had come from the same place. This was her first conscious awareness of a bodily connection—or any intimate fantasies. The perception of a bodily connection provided a means of experiencing and expressing emotional intimacy.

B had great difficulty talking about her wishes for closeness or love for the analyst. Occasionally she could express these wishes in the form of fantasies of stroking the analyst's body or genitals, feeling it was like her own body. The way she could feel close was through this specific experience, with the thought that they could have the same sensations, because their bodies were the same. She also had a fantasy of being inside the analyst's body and thereby feeling protected. This feeling of sameness was important. She felt she would feel what the analyst felt or would feel and that would convey closeness. It was as if she could feel close through a sensual identification.

I will describe a patient whose conflicts and wishes and her relationship with her mother were expressed through her feelings about her body and also determined the athletic activities she did.

N is a 50-year-old divorced woman. She came to treatment in a panic, after having arranged to see her primary care physician, a woman, for a routine visit. An earlier period of treatment had helped lift her depression related to the divorce. She had been active and athletic as a teenager and young adult. She had resumed a program of exercise, changed her diet, and lost considerable weight. Her body shape had changed. Friends and acquaintances commented on this. "It was more like the body I wanted," she said. This created anxiety. It was too sexual.

Previously she had dressed in large shapeless clothing and now, having lost so much weight, she could change what she wore but she was terribly anxious about showing her body in this new shape. It was this that frightened her when she thought about going to see the doctor. It would be a statement the doctor would see. She felt particularly terrified because her legs, now slim, didn't touch each other when she walked. Later she said that that made her feel "incredibly sexual." Earlier, while the divorce arrangements were in process, she had had feelings of nausea. She had felt "dirty, unable to get clean." The only thing that helped was to eat enormous quantities of food. When she began to feel better and lost weight she said she felt she had an "edge to my body, I feel it press against my clothes. I feel my lungs expand. When I'm heavy I don't feel that way. When I'm thinner I have to feel the feelings in my body. I can't pretend." Taking her body seriously also meant taking care of her needs.

As we talked about her feelings about her body, a history of long-standing sexual abuse by her grandfather emerged. It began when she was a small child, with touching under the guise of affectionate fondling, and then went on into adulthood with explicit sexual activities. She felt she had no choice but to comply. She recalled memories of the country house where some of this took place and her dread of hidden places there. This was also translated to dread about her body. She had told her mother about this. Her mother consistently refused to believe that this abuse had occurred and said that "it didn't happen." N felt her mother's extensive denial of reality in other ways as well.

Her grandfather was a prominent man. N believed that her mother had experienced the same abuse and had denied its meaning or refused to acknowledge it. At the same time, N had a hunger for affection and was saddened by her grandfather's and her mother's coldness.

Over time, she described her mother's "denial of the body" and reality in many ways. When the patient's father was dying, her mother refused to believe it. Although he was hospitalized with serious circulatory and respiratory problems, she urged him to get up and made future plans for them as if he could move directly from his bed. She refused medication for herself or any family member who was ill. She fell and injured her foot and refused to see a doctor, continuing with plans for distant travel, limping and needing a wheelchair to get on the airplane. A fracture was diagnosed on her return. She described an incident the week before that distressed her. A clear sexual overtone and flirtation had developed between a babysitter and a younger child that they had all seen. Her mother thought nothing was amiss.

Having a slim body with a shape she liked gave rise to painful and guilty feelings and memories, not only of her grandfather but of a period of intense sexual activity in adolescence, in the context of her parents' frequent moves and disregard of her feelings of abandonment. She also felt guilty about other times when she had many sexual relationships. The "body surrounded by a wall" was some protection, but left her feeling "crumpled," hiding herself and uncomfortable.

The confusion about the validity of her perceptions and her "reality" compared with her mother's pronouncements was also expressed by her feeling confused about her sense of separateness, her plans and hopes for the future. She sometimes said she felt "doomed." "The knowledge that the way things are is not how they are defined, described or even lived by my mother does not save me from the stuckness." This was also expressed by a feeling of "being stuck in my body."

In adolescence, N once told her grandfather that she would like to enter his field. He said that girls couldn't do this. They only got married and had children. N felt humiliated and as if she were told "you are good only for sex." She recognized his generational and societal stereotyping and the depreciation of women this represented, but felt not only the personal rebuff but also as if she were a whore.

Her mother was a slim "straight up and down" woman who dressed in what the daughter called "transparent" clothing. Her career had occasioned many moves during N and her sister's childhood. She and N's father frequently ignored the wishes of both daughters, such as sending N to a boarding school at a distant location, which the mother preferred rather than one she wanted. She bought clothes that she rather than the daughter liked.

Her mother's denial of the reality of the sexual abuse, of much of N's experience, had a profound effect. She cannot hold on to a consistent feeling about her body. She said, "My body in clothes, sloshing about or feeling the edge of the fabric and learning my edge from the seams in the cloth." At the time of a visit from her sister to her mother, she said, "I feel sideswiped," because her mother and sister appeared to be in "a bubble" that entirely excluded her. Her feeling of abandonment and nonexistence was thus expressed in the absence of feelings of bodily integrity.

Recently she described that she is more able to differentiate her mother's point of view from her own sense of what is real. However, the longing to have something from her mother can override this. "My yearning to be within her world overshadowed whatever affronts there are to myself or my world or the common world (reality), which I then set aside." The fear of doing irreparable damage to the relationship and losing her mother if she really differentiates herself is powerful. "More reason for me to want to make sure that I am translating my world into words that fit into my mother's world." So, to have her own life is dangerous. To have her own body in its slim form "with an edge" is dangerous, both for its sexuality and for the implications of aloneness and loss.

Her mother's denial of the sexual abuse by her grandfather and denial of the sexuality in the child's experience with the caretaker also serves to convey her mother's disapproval of her sexuality. So, to please her mother, her own sexuality, not to speak of her aggression, must also be denied.

She feels she sometimes hovers anxiously over her children and her mother and gives up some of her own initiative. When she does sometimes feel she can be without her mother, or children, she feels she can "stand tall and be strong." At times when she feels strong and remembers past periods of physical activity and achievement, which are expressions of aggression, she both hears an inner voice that is constricting and inhibiting and interprets any outer voice of caution as inhibiting. This can be her grandfather saying she can't be ambitious or a projection of her mother inhibiting aggression and sexuality. It is expressed in bodily terms.

Aging

Individual variations in life experience and physical capability make it difficult to generalize about aging. Unlike early development, the milestones are not age related in the same consistent way. Benedek (1970a) saw parenthood as "timeless" with parents "clinging to the status parenthood gave them" (p. 185). She thought that developmental phases in the child reactivate in the parent conflicts originating in the developmental phase of the parent. For example, she thought that with the daughter's pregnancy, the mother can reexperience her own pregnancies. When the mother grows older, there is no model in the daughter, and it is more likely that she recalls her own mother's aging. Old feelings of loss and anxiety can emerge. Some older mothers hold on to their independence to a point. That may make their children anxious. They can become protective, controlling, as they may be with their own children.

Some generally accepted ideas about aging have been subject to changes because of new data and the increasing life span. Parents, including mothers of adult daughters, are more active than a few generations ago. More women are healthy, working, and are physically and sexually active. There is not an inevitable postmenopausal decline in sexual interest. The greatest barrier to an active sexual life in older women is the unavailability of partners.

How does this affect the daughters? Competitive feelings can take on different dynamics. The older mother or grandmother is not necessarily seen as nonsexual and can be felt as a competitor.

There are some widely held views about the role reversal that is said to occur between aging parents and their children. Changes with aging place caretaking demands on children, which can reawaken old oedipal issues. Even when the elderly mother develops an illness, or dementia, and needs caretaking and life management by the daughter, old anxieties can remain.

Grunes (1984) challenges the inevitability of this role reversal. He describes specific impasses that occur between aging parents and adult children. He believes that psychopathology can develop for the first time in elderly people and does not necessarily emerge from early conflicts alone. Elderly parents resent being infantilized and at the same time may feel more dependent on adult children and are afraid to risk losing their care by being critical.

The old conflicts about autonomy and control can resurface. Aging involves losses of physical strength and sometimes health. Some ego functions such as memory and judgment are diminished. How the adult child responds can be crucial. Preserving the "self" of the parent in the face of these challenges is important.

G is a 64-year-old married woman who was very successful professionally as the head of an institution. She has a grown daughter and a granddaughter. When her mother became significantly unable to care for herself with some memory loss and confusion, G had difficulty arranging moving her mother to an assisted living facility near her from the expensive care in a distant city. With all the obvious benefits—financial, geographic, and emotional—of having her mother closer and more protected, she was very anxious about the possibility that her mother, misconstruing the move, would become explosively angry. She described a lifelong fear of her mother's anger, which reduced her to tears even at this time. Old anxieties and her adaptations of placating and avoidance remained as vulnerabilities.

Sometimes new adaptations can be surprisingly gratifying. M, an 85-year-old mother and grandmother lost her husband of 60 years. It became clear that she could not function on her own. When she moved to a nursing home, her daughter was afraid that she would become depressed, but the facility was closer and more frequent visits were possible. The nursing home aides decided to persuade M to wear makeup, which she had never done. She was delighted to see herself as more a part of the mainstream of conventional femininity—a surprise to her daughter and her son-in-law. It appeared no longer necessary to define herself as a nonconformist individual to retain her self-esteem. How does this relate to early dementia? How does it relate to the new social context and her daughter's support, having lost her identity as a wife and part of her husband's world? She had had an early identity as an independent, energetic, creative, and rebellious person, which remained through many years of immigration, moves, and adaptation to many changes. The loss of her husband, her home, her actual independence, may have made being taken into another community welcome.

It will be interesting to see how longer life spans, probably longer periods of widowhood, and a greater range of life patterns affect adult mother–daughter relationships. These are, of course moderated by class, subcultural, and geographic factors. There are potentially different constellations of mutual adulthood that may become clearer with more careful study and description.

REFERENCES

Auchinclos, E. & Michels, R. (1989), The impact of middle age on ambitions and ideals. In: *The Middle Years,* eds. J. Oldham & R. Liebert. New Haven, CT: Yale University Press, pp. 40–57.

Balsam, R. (1996), The pregnant mother and the body image of the daughter, *J. Amer. Psychoanal. Assn.* (Female Development Supplement), 44:401–442.

_____ (2003), The mother within the mother. In: *The Inner World of the Mother,* ed. D. Mendell & P. Turrini. Madison, CT: Psychosocial Press, pp. 71–97.

Barnett, R. (2004), Women and multiple roles: Myth and reality, *Harv. Rev. Psychiatr.,* 12:158–164.

Benedek, T. (1970), Parenthood during the life cycle. In: *Parenthood, Its Psychology and Psychopathology,* eds. J. Anthony & T. Benedek. Boston, MA: Little, Brown & Co., pp. 185–206.

Bernstein, P. (2004), Mothers and daughters from today's psychoanalytic perspective, *Psychoanal. Inq.* 24:601–628.

Bibring, G. (1959), Some considerations of the psychological processes in pregnancy, *The Psychoanalytical Study of the Child,* 14:113–121. New York: International Universitites Press.

_____, Dwyer, T. Huntington, D. & Valensstein, A. (1961), A study of the psychological processes in pregnancy and of the earliest mother–child relationship, *The Psychoanalytical Study of the Child,* 16:9–72. New Haven, CT: Yale University Press.

Chodorow, N. (1978/1999), *The Reproduction of Mothering: Psychoanalysis and the Sociology of Gender.* New Haven, CT: Yale University Press. New Preface in 1999.

Dahl, E. K. (1995) Daughters and mothers: Aspects of the representational world during adolescence, *The Psychoanalytic Study of the Child,* 50:187–204. New Haven, CT: Yale University Press.

Erikson, E. (1950), Eight ages of man. In: *Childhood and Society.* New York, NY: Norton, pp. 247–274.

Freud, S. (1913), Totem and Taboo. *Standard Edition,* 13:1–161. London: Hogarth Press.

Grunes, J. (1984), Parenthood issues in the aging process. In: *Parenthood: A Psychodynamic Perspective,* eds. R. Cohen, B. Cohler & S. Weissman. New York: Guilford Press.

Hoffman, L. (2004), When daughter becomes mother: Inferences from multiple dyadic parent–child groups, *Psychoanal. Inq.*, 24:629–656.

Holtzman, D. & Kulish, N. (2000), The feminization of the female Oedipus Complex, Part I, *J. Amer. Psychoanal. Assn.*, 48:1413–1437.

Jaques, E. (1980), The midlife crisis. In: *The Course of Life, Vol. III: Adulthood and the Aging Process,* eds. S. Greenspan & G. Pollock. Washington, DC: National Institute of Mental Health, pp. 1–23.

Jessner, L, Weigert, E. & Foy, J. (1970), The development of parental attitudes during pregnancy. In: *Parenthood, Its Psychology and Psychopathology,* eds. J. Anthony & T. Benedek. Boston, MA: Little, Brown & Co., pp. 209–244.

Kulish, N. & Holtzman, D. (1998), Persephone, the loss of virginity and the female Oedipus complex, *Int. J. Psychoanal.*, 79:57–71.

Miller, J. B. (1973), *Psychoanalysis and Women.* New York: Bremmer, Nagel.

Pines, D. (1997), The relevance of early psychic development to pregnancy and abortion. In: *Female Experience,* eds. J. Raphael-Leff & R. Perlberg. London: Routledge.

Schrier, D., Tompsett, M. & Schrier, L. (2004), Adult mother–daughter relationships: A review of the theoretical and research literature, *J. Amer. Acad of Psychoanal. & Dynamic Psychiat.*, 32:91–115.

54 Clark Road
Brookline, MA 02445
malkah_notman@hms.harvard.edu

Epilogue

WE HAVE PRESENTED PORTRAITS OF WOMEN—YOUNG, MIDDLE-AGED, and old—bonded across the generations. We see them struggling with each other; envying and admiring, imitating and competing, weeping with and for each other; fighting, tempting, arousing and ignoring; subjugating, dominating, pleading and domineering; hating, scorning, hurting, blending and annihilating; losing, finding, grieving for each other, teasing, laughing, forgiving each other and loving, ever loving each other—sometimes too much, sometimes too little, but always, always deeply affected by each other's resonances. We have presented their therapists' discovering them, musing about them, challenging them, helping them, inadvertently hindering them, supporting them, interpreting them to themselves and always thinking about them searchingly.

We hope that these two volumes, which we have immensely enjoyed putting together, working over with our authors and assembling with the help of the The Analytic Press staff, will enrich the contemporary psychoanalytic scene of female developmental theory and practice in our field and keep the excitement of this primordial conversation going that is about mothers and daughters.

Rosemary H. Balsam, M.D.
Ruth S. Fischer, M.D.
Issue Editors

For Product Safety Concerns and Information please contact our EU representative GPSR@taylorandfrancis.com
Taylor & Francis Verlag GmbH, Kaufingerstraße 24, 80331 München, Germany

www.ingramcontent.com/pod-product-compliance
Lightning Source LLC
LaVergne TN
LVHW022051200926
848481LV00003B/865